Meditation's Secret Treasure

Awakening to the Mystic World

An American Tao Book

The *American Tao* books, of which *Meditation's Secret Treasure* is the first, are unlike anything you will ever read. They present the true story of what happened when a skeptical, spiritual neophyte sat down to begin a daily practice of meditation and somehow slid through a crack between worlds, ultimately ending up in a strange new psychic dimension of the Soul. Unbeknownst to him, he had been called. He had become the accidental mystic, a traveller of worlds.

In repeated visits over an extended period, the author experienced over seventy strange visions and apparitions. These led him on a journey across multiple realms and worlds, ultimately taking him into the celestial chambers of a mysterious white-bearded being, where a final secret was revealed. The complete chronicle of the author's travels is presented in this series.

And every bit of it is true!

This book gets you started. The author presents his story so that you will be prepared for yours. His story paves the way for your own travels, by showing you the kinds of initiation events that can signal the beginning of a major shift in consciousness. Using his own experiences, he describes how visions test and prepare the practitioner for travel to different worlds and the onset of new revelations. He shows how childhood events can summon you onto the mystic path, so that you can look for similar experiences in your own earlier life. The author presents all the information you need to start a meditative practice, including the philosophy and mystical teachings of Taoism, and shows you how to record and analyze your experiences to gain a deeper understanding.

The Story of an Errant Seeker

When I began this endeavor I was not a mystic. In fact, I was as far from a mystic as you could get, as you can clearly see from my *before* picture. But I kept myself busy, running here and there, hiding from my calling. I was always seeking something, always in pursuit of the next job, the next title, the next distinction, etc. I just didn't know what I was looking for. Only meditation would provide the answer.

Over the years, I picked up degrees from some of the best universities, including a BS from MIT, a PhD in philosophy from Harvard and an MBA from UC Berkeley.

With these in hand, I worked in biotech as an engineer at Agilent Technology and Silicon Genetics, a researcher in space biology at NASA Ames, a computer programmer at several start-ups, and a philosophy professor at Stanford University. I've managed engineers at IBM and Silicon Graphics. I have eight patents in computer science. I worked as a computer animator and digital artist.

I still train as a Chinese martial artist, having accumulated boxes of dusty gold medals in local and national competitions, along with a couple of all-around championships in the internal martial arts.

Looking back at all this, I had to wonder what in the world was I looking for. What unfulfilled desire was driving me? But then, magically, I somehow stumbled on a method that opened doors to the hidden worlds of the Soul, pulling me in. All these other things turned out to be just so much smoke and mirrors. My background may not have prepared me for the journey I was to undertake, but it did help me tell the tale of what I encountered along the way, so that I could begin to mark the trails for you to follow on your own journeys. I welcome you to my story and, perhaps, the beginning of yours as well.

Meditation's Secret Treasure

Awakening to the Mystic World

An American Tao Book

S.Strasnick, PhD

Mystic Tao Publishing

ISBN-13: 978-0-9976471-0-5
ISBN-10: 0997647108

Cover Art, Book Design & Graphics:
Steven Strasnick

Editing:
Nell Griscom

Printed in the United States of America

Library of Congress Control Number: 2016909343
Mystic Tao Publishing

Mystic Tao
Publishing

stevos2000@icloud.com
Santa Cruz, CA

Some Words of Warning

"There's nothing more irritating than Americans
hoping to locate their inner Tao," Dad said.

-- Marisha Pessl, p. 165 in
Special Topics in Calamity Physics

". . . except, perhaps, when they find it
and have to tell you all about it."

-- The Author, with apologies, in
Meditation's Secret Treasure

"Don't say I didn't say I didn't warn you."

-- Taylor Swift in *Blank Space*

Acknowledgements

A lot of people helped bring me to this point in my life, but there are several I wish to thank here: first of all, my wife Katie, who provides constant support and nurturing, not only during these intense periods of writing, but all other times as well, my editor Nell Griscom, who has been patiently teaching me to say the same things in fewer words and relax around my tenses, and finally Kitano, who showed me what a helping spirit really is.

Table of Contents

Preface

On December 27th, 2013 I sat down to begin what I hoped would become a daily practice of meditation, not suspecting that my world was about to change irrevocably. Within minutes of closing my eyes I witnessed the first of many strange visions and apparitions that would visit me over the next year and a half, the vast majority occurring within the first three months before starting to diminish in frequency. I had somehow opened the floodgates to the worlds of my unconscious.

At first, surprisingly, I did not consider these experiences unusual or deserving of further study. Like you, I've learned to accept my nighttime dreams as a normal part of life. These just seemed a kind of daytime dream. If anything, I found them entertaining. I simply assumed that they, like dreams, were something that happened when you slipped into an alternative state of consciousness, something best experienced and then quickly forgotten. After all, that was the advice offered by all the introductory books on meditation I looked at.

Over the next couple of months, as these experiences continued to accumulate, my perspective started to change. My curiosity began to grow. Was what was happening to me typical? I talked to many long-term meditators and asked them about their experiences. I dove into the mystical literature to see if I could discover historical antecedents to my experiences. While none of the people I talked to reported anything remotely similar, I did find examples in history of mystics who had.

Things grew even stranger for me on March 24th, 2014. On that day, approximately 45 minutes into my meditation session, I experienced what I subsequently came to refer to as "The Awakening." Several things occurred simultaneously. It began with my awareness suddenly snapping back into the ordinary world from whatever kind of trance state I had been in. The first thing I noticed was that the CD player in my room that had been playing soft meditation music was now skipping wildly, like an old fashioned phonograph, repeatedly jumping back to the same spot, in an endless loop. The volume also seemed much louder. I thought the room was shaking. My body definitely was.

As more physical sensations returned to me, I realized that I had been hyperventilating, breathing dramatically quicker than I normally did during meditation. More significantly, I felt a torrent of energy streaming into the top of my head and down my spine, where it seemed to settle in my lower abdominal region, below my navel. I did not experience this energy as painful, though it was certainly intense. Words don't really suffice, but the best way to describe it was to call it a physical experience of ecstatic bliss. In my readings I had learned about the phenomenon of the Kundalini experience, in which energy reportedly shot up the practitioner's spine. This seemed like a variant of that experience, a kind of reverse Kundalini. The physical aftershocks from this experience reverberated through my meditation sessions for the next week. The psychic aftershocks, which carried over into my everyday life, lasted much longer.

Since that event, I have often calmed myself with the thought that I knew "why the Buddha smiled." At times I considered that this phrase was a good title for the account I soon felt compelled to write. Because of that event and others that followed it, I finally accepted both the uniqueness and the strangeness of what was happening to me. The rationalist in me felt the accumulated body of all these experiences deserved further study and documentation. This work was the result.

This account is as factual as I can make it. No matter how strange my story might seem at times, the events it describes actually took place. It chronicles what happened to me during the initial stages of my meditative practice, along with my subsequent attempts to understand the meaning and interrelationships of these strange experiences. I tell my story so that you will be better prepared for yours, when that day comes.

I know my task will be challenging, since I am trying to investigate the visionary realms of the unconscious using the analytical tools of the rational mind. Some readers will no doubt be more comfortable in one of these domains than the other. But sometimes looking at things through new lens enables us to see things we never saw before. That was my experience.

Both because of the sheer number of visions I experienced and the evolving forms of their narratives, I will present my account in multiple volumes. This first book gets you started. My story paves the way for your own travels, by showing you the kinds of initiation events that signal the beginning of a major shift in consciousness. Using my own experiences, I describe how visions test and prepare the practitioner for travels to different worlds and the onset of new revelations. I show how childhood events can summon you onto the mystic path, so that you can look for similar experiences in your own earlier life. I present all the information you need to start a meditative practice, including the philosophy and mystical teachings of Taoism, and show you how to record and analyze your own experiences to gain a deeper understanding.

In my second book, which will be published later this year, I continue the story of my journey as I leave the Home realm of my initial visions and begin a circuit through the three levels of the mystic Worlds. I'll chronicle my shamanic journeys from the familiar surroundings of the Surface World down to the primitive regions of the Under World, where I witness strange beings and rituals. I then travel upwards to the Mountain and High Desert realms of the Upper World, where I undergo a series of trials and tribulations before receiving a magical key and entry into strange societies. This book serves as a guidebook to the mystic Worlds.

The third and final volume will detail my eventual passage to the Celestial realms, where I experienced my final revelation before returning to Earth transfigured. It will describe in detail the flow of the different internal energies that appeared after "The Awakening" and the associated series of visionary events that followed in the external world. These led to a series of visions that fragmented my self into multiple identities before transforming it for my final ascension to the Upper World. I will end my account with a description of everything I have learned in the course of my journeys and discuss the formative role of Spirit in our lives.

In spite of my many strange experiences or perhaps because of them, meditation has now become an uneventful part of my daily routine. Gone are the strange incursions that were once such a regular part of my practice. My unconscious still speaks to me, but now only in whispers. Whatever tale my unconscious had chosen to share with me has, at least for now, come to an end. All that remains to discover is what I could learn from it.

-- Santa Cruz, May 2016

Foreword

The Secret Treasure

Hidden deep within us all is a treasure of immense richness. This treasure is not the key to wealth, or to psychic power, or to perfect health. It is not the secret to longevity or intelligence or even to lasting happiness. It won't make you famous and it certainly won't make you any thinner.

Not much of a treasure you say? Then these books may not be for you.

For those of you who are still reading, this treasure conceals a secret that once revealed will bring with it something of such immeasurable value that all these other attainments will seem like mere trifles. And the good news is that many of these other attainments will, though unsought, appear like so many surprise gifts along the path to its discovery.

Through the millennia many religions and philosophers have written about the search for this treasure. They have given it many different names, often describing it as the search for our true nature. Many seek it as the Self or Soul. I view the path to its discovery as the Tao. I will use these names and more to refer to this quest. But the names we use won't tell us anything about the treasure we seek.

The Good News

Surprisingly, the method for finding it is simple. All you have to do is nothing. Just sit yourself down in a quiet place and do nothing. That's it. The rest will follow. Of course, sometimes the simplest thing is the hardest to do. Within my account, you will discover everything you need to begin your own journey. I call it the Practice, for that's all it takes.

The catch, of course, is that while the method for its discovery is simple, what you will experience along the way is unknown. It's like that famous journey of a thousand miles. Take a few steps. Repeat. But what will happen to you when you make this journey?

What sights will you see? What will you feel? The same questions apply to this Practice.

The truth is no one really knows the answer because we are all different. None of us will start or end our journeys in the same way. We all must follow our own paths. Our experiences along the way will be different, shaped by who we are and what we are destined to learn. That's what's so unique about each of our journeys.

Meditation?

"Oh," you say, "You're talking about meditation. I've heard this sales pitch before." You are skeptical. You have many questions. Could I do this? Do I have the patience? Is it worth the effort? Do I have the time? The answer to all these questions is "yes."

So what really prevents you from beginning this simple journey? It is not just that you still have more questions. It is also that you still have fears, and probably a mix of several different ones at that: a fear of the unknown, a fear of losing your most tightly held beliefs, a fear of what you might learn were your secrets to be revealed to you.

Or maybe it is the greatest fear of them all: the fear that, despite all your best efforts, nothing much will happen, that when you finally open that buried secret vault, you will find nothing more than some dirt and empty old bottles. For there lurks your deepest fear: not that you had wasted your time, but that your hidden Self had judged you and found you wanting, unworthy to serve as its vessel or taste its fruits.

I know these fears. I too have had all these misgivings, which is probably why so much of my life had to pass before I was ready to take the plunge. But many a day since then has been touched with the sense of wonder I know now had been missing from my life. It was like seeing a formerly black and white world in color for the first time.

A True Account

Like you perhaps, I had read many of the books and accounts about meditation. Meditation is, after all, a hot topic right now. It's "trending." No matter where you turn, you hear about the importance of being "mindful" and how "guided" meditations can bring the benefits of meditation to anyone, all in just a few minutes a day. They'll probably promise you some combination of those things I listed in that first paragraph. Hey, there's probably an app to make this easier for you.

I read the accounts and was skeptical. It all sounded counterfeit to me. Was American culture doing to meditation what it had done to yoga and every other Eastern discipline it had gotten its hands on? Hollowing it out to make it ready for mass consumption? Turning it into a commercial fad? Monetizing it? I had to find out for myself what was real and what was just marketing hype.

Where could you find an authentic account of meditation, one that was not a warmed over rehash of some guru's mystical experiences from some far off land or time, told in metaphors culturally inaccessible to you? This was the challenge I took upon myself, to produce a true first-person account of where meditation could lead, one written right here in contemporary America.

Not a Mystic

"But I'm no mystic," you say. "I don't believe in any of this stuff." That's not a problem. It might even be a requirement. You won't be surprised if you're not a skeptic. And you won't believe in the reality of what you encounter unless you are surprised, unless your worldview is shaken to its very core.

I was like you. When I began this endeavor I was not a mystic. In fact, I was as far from a mystic as you could get. I was a down-to-earth, skeptical spiritual neophyte who only believed in what he could see or touch. That hasn't changed. Through meditation you will be able to experience a whole new world of sights and sounds and textures. Meditation doesn't immediately change everything about you, only what really matters, deep down. Much of your external personality has been baked in, the result of a lifetime of inertia. But changes will come, slowly bubbling to the surface.

No Secrets

Unlike others who have had similar experiences, I don't believe in keeping what I have seen secret. I have no guru to whom I have sworn allegiance or whose rules of silence I must follow. No authority figure or intermediary stands between me and the truths I seek or the insights I hope to reveal.

In these pages I will present my story as it happened, unvarnished and unwashed. You can make your own judgment about what it all means. You are the ultimate judge of whether my words hint at deeper truths. My hope is that I can find among my readers many who can help me authenticate the validity of what I experienced.

I wrote these chronicles to describe not only the surprising things that happened to one neophyte practitioner (me), but also to show what might await you as well. With this account you can travel with me on my journeys, as I visit strange realms and encounter enigmatic phenomena and characters along the way. That will give you a taste of the kinds of experiences potentially available to you, should you decide this is a type of journey you would want for yourself.

Whether my words will resonate will depend entirely on you and your experiences. Like a writer for a travel guide, I can only point out the potential sites of interest and provide a context for their understanding. Ultimately, the sites will have to speak for themselves.

Come with Me

I invite you to come with me as I recount my inner journey. I will act as your host, welcoming you as a guest inside my mind. There you can witness my attempts to distill whatever meaning I could from my visions, sometimes even while I was still in their clutches. You can share in the mysteries I confronted and see what they might reveal about the nature of the Self.

I hope my adventures will pique your interest and awaken a desire in you, as they had in me, to trek further into the unknown. At the very least, maybe this account will help you believe in what you already suspect in your heart to be true, something that calls to you now, as it did me.

I know we have very different backgrounds and experiences. But despite these differences, there is a deep core we all share. That is why wondrous experiences await you too, if you are willing to open the doors to their hiding places. Whatever form these experiences take, they will be uniquely yours. They will change you in ways you cannot imagine.

All you have to do is open yourself up to the possibility that something totally unexpected is awaiting discovery in you as it was in me. It turns out that what so many spiritual teachers have said is true: *all you have to do is believe.* Even opening yourself to the possibility of belief may be enough. The rest will follow. Amazingly, you can do all this from the comfort of your own easy chair.

I end this foreword with a quotation from chapter 47 of the *Tao-Te-Ching*, the classic work of Taoist philosophy written by the sage Lao Tzu in the 6th century BC. I will be returning often to this work to add some Taoist context to accounts of my meditational practice and visionary journeys, since I have come to recognize in it and other writings on Taoist meditation many elements similar to my own experiences. Indeed, the fact of this recognition was one of the major reasons that drove my belief that something profound had happened to me.

-- *Santa Cruz, December 2014*

"Without going outside your door,
You can know everything under Heaven.
Without looking out your window,
You can see the Way of Heaven.
But the further you travel,
The less you will know.
Therefore, the sages did not travel
And yet they knew.
They did not see,
And yet they understood.
They did not act,
And yet they succeeded."

Fig. 1. Shall We Begin?

Journey's Prelude

Mystical incursions, the Trickster's challenge,
Taoist philosophy, and beginning the
Practice of meditation

1. What Meditation Had Wrought

Day 113: *A Shaggy Dog Story*

The Enchanted Frog

The day started out like any other in the lovely seaside town of Santa Cruz, California. It was a Friday morning on April 18th, 2014, a little before 9 o'clock. It was my 113th day since starting to sit in meditation. I had just finished my morning practice, having spent a comfortable hour enveloped in warm vibrating energy. This was a new experience I had been enjoying every morning for the last several weeks in the aftermath of the mysterious experience I called "The Awakening." But today more was afoot cosmically than just another quick dip in an ethereal tide pool.

There's an old folk tale about a frog and a pot of water that is apropos to my story. Put a frog in a container of tepid water and gradually increase the water's temperature until the water boils. If the changes in temperature are gradual enough, the story goes, the frog won't jump out until it's too late. In point of fact, frogs will jump out of any pot of water the first chance they get. But the story is a parable for the way small changes can creep up on you unnoticed until it's too late and something irrevocable happens. It's similar to what happens when you slowly add grains of sand to a big pile and then the whole thing comes crashing down.

So there I was, the metaphorical frog in this story, hopping my way down the High Street hill, across the pedestrian bridge over Highway 1, and about to cross Mission Plaza Park on my way to Mission Street and downtown Santa Cruz. My thoughts, when they occurred, were focused on serious things.

Unlike recent bright and sunny mornings, this morning was grey and foggy. A swirling damp mist hugged the ground. Looking back on that day, it's easy to see how things had seemed a little off, a little too quiet. It was as if the world had lost its focus.

2

Fig. 2. Entering Mission Plaza Park

The park too felt different that morning. Usually there were many people around as this was a fairly well trafficked area. Many buildings were adjacent to the park, including a large Holy Cross church complex and school, the Mission Santa Cruz, and a bunch of houses of rather mixed lineage. There was a very lovely Victorian there at the corner of one of Santa Cruz's busiest streets and a bus stop on that same street. The park also had its own contingent of local characters, but not this morning. This morning, no one was about, neither man nor beast.

But I, as the happy yet clueless amphibian, was as fuzzy as the day. Perhaps I was luxuriating in the feel of the damp air against my skin. Or maybe I was still basking in the residual glow from the morning's meditation. Unconcerned, I headed into the park on the diagonal path towards the fountain in the park's center. I only made it a few steps into its interior.

Day Break

Suddenly the day awoke fitfully from its slumber and found its voice. This took the form of a very loud and continually blasting horn. No tentative beeps these, mind you. A nonstop cacophony of sound pierced the quiet morning air. Still, I found this to be no cause for alarm. It was probably just someone a little out of sync with the mood of the day. Too much caffeine and too little patience were a bad combination.

If you've lived in California for any prolonged period of time, you might be familiar with the following experience. You're going about your normal business when suddenly the ground starts to shake. Initially you think, "Oh, it's probably a truck or a train going by, nothing to worry about." But the shaking doesn't stop, so now you're thinking, "Just another silly earthquake, maybe a 3 or 4." But then the shaking still doesn't stop, and the room begins to sway, and stuff starts falling down. At this point you are no longer thinking but frantically heading for the exit.

Well, it felt like that. I wanted to head for the exit. The damn horn, like the 1989 Loma Prieta quake, didn't stop. It went on . . . and on . . . and on. And like a psychic quake, cracks started to open up in my view of everyday reality. Were I the proverbial frog in this story, the water in my pot would be starting to boil.

I looked around, pivoting in a clockwise circle: right, back, left, front. Someone watching from afar would have wondered why this guy was spinning in circles. I found the source of the sound pretty quickly. It was a squarish looking older model sedan parked next to the curb on Sylvar Avenue about 20 feet to my right.

I looked around again to see if anyone else was reacting to what had now become a fairly insistent and strident clamor for attention. I expected to see someone emerge from one of the many buildings surrounding the park, but no one came. This puzzled me. Surely someone must be hearing this. This couldn't be a normal occurrence around here, could it?

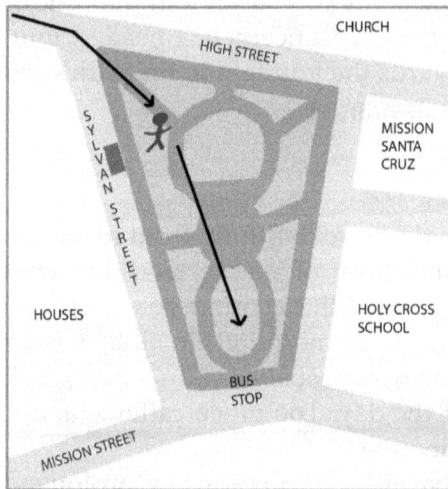

Fig. 3. My Path through the Park

I left the path and started across the grass towards the source. I was worried someone might be in trouble. As I got a little closer, I saw a woman perched behind the steering wheel. She was wearing a ruffled old sweater, with long unkempt brown hair. At least she wasn't a child in distress. She turned her head towards me and gave me the strangest looking smile. It was both smug and impish. All the while she continued to lean on the horn.

Did I know this woman? Maybe she was one of Santa Cruz's many colorful characters. While I watched, she seemed to grow more vehement in her efforts. The sound modulated higher in pitch and intensity, as if the horn was protesting its overuse. Was the thing broken? Why wouldn't it stop?

The Tell Tale Tail

I approached even closer. Then, as when two plates deep in the earth fracture, causing the ground to jump, my vision flickered. The illusion before my eyes shattered. Something snapped.

Where before there had been an unkempt, longhaired woman, there now sat a large, mischievous looking sheepdog. She had a light tan face and long brown ears. She was still relentlessly pressing on the horn, but with paws on the steering wheel instead of hands. She continued smiling at me with that same silly grin on her face.

I was uncertain about the shaggy beast's motivation or what message the universe was trying to send me. I thought better of trying to engage her in conversation. Maybe that was my mistake. Who knows what I might have learned. All I could manage was to shake my head a few times, mutter and walk away.

I did look around again to see if there were any witnesses to this strange encounter. As before, none made themselves known. I felt like the victim of someone's cosmic practical joke or the protagonist in a hastily written science fiction story. As in the old *Candid Camera* TV shows, the true perpetrators remained hidden.

I retraced my steps through the grass, rejoining the paved path. The unbroken wail of the horn followed me as I passed the fountain and headed out of the park. At that point, perhaps because it was apparent I was intent on leaving, the honking stopped. Finally. How long had it been? Was it 30 seconds, 45 seconds, a minute, longer? It had seemed like a long time. But time, like the day, seemed a little slippery too.

Fig. 4. A Likeness of my Shaggy Dog

I paused and looked back over my shoulder towards the car one more time. Then I abruptly turned to leave, intending to put this all behind me. This might have caused some consternation on the part of my observer for I was suddenly hit with three quick blasts from the rear: two quick taps, a pause, and then a final tap. Apparently my shaggy nemesis knew more than just how to lean against a horn. Clever girl.

Commentary

Honk If You Heard This

Strangely, this event didn't provoke much of a reaction from me at the time. There was nothing in my gut, no surge of adrenalin. The best I could offer for commentary at the time was a puzzled shake of my head. Why had I experienced no reaction to this strange encounter? Had my four months of meditation turned this into just another walk in the park?

A skeptic might point out that while my morning's adventure with the shaggy dog was a good story, it was no earth-shattering event. Like the punch line to the similarly named joke goes: "He's not that shaggy." Apparently, dogs honking car horns were not unheard of events in the new globally connected world in which we live. I discovered this later that day. The Internet was full of stories and videos of dogs engaged in this and other bizarre kinds of behavior. Just try 'Googling' "dogs honking horns." I did. You get pages of results.

Even my misidentification of the species of the car's occupant was not unprecedented. Our minds are known to play tricks on us when confronted with novel situations. And there are novel situations aplenty in the world. Physicists are always telling us that no matter how seemingly improbable an event may be, there was always a finite possibility of it happening, sooner or later, somewhere in the universe. Maybe somewhere was here today.

So, yes, bizarre things do regularly happen in the world. Maybe our everyday reality was a little more "cracked" than we believed, leaving it vulnerable to incursions of mischief leaking in from other realms. Was that what was happening here? As my niece Alix succinctly observed after patiently sitting through my convoluted account of this event, "I was with you *until* the 'honk,' 'honk,' (pause), 'honk.'"

The Miracle of the Mundane

From my perspective, this incident did cross a line in the sand, even for Santa Cruz, which has plenty of sand and a little weirdness to spare. It was one thing to have strange encounters in the cozy living room of one's own head, such as when dreaming or meditating, or even right after waking up, when residues of cosmic mischief were still bouncing around. It was quite another for the extended train of these accumulated antics to gather enough momentum to jump the tracks, breaking from the inner realm into the light of day.

You might say the day had successfully carried out the trick of the magician: taking the "extra" out of the extraordinary and, while keeping you distracted, slipping it into the ordinary. Surprise! So what if the day had blurred the differences between the usual and the unusual, the normal and the abnormal, the miraculous and the mundane? Apparently I was OK with that. The ability to see *everyday life as miraculous* was one of the gifts bestowed by a successful Practice, even if it was something that took some getting used to. Having already been exposed to so many of the mind's hijinks, I guess I knew it was only a matter of time before some started sneaking into my everyday life.

Sitting in meditation showed me I had been conditioned from a very early age to ignore the mysteries hovering at the edges of my consciousness, or at least had been thoroughly desensitized to them. It allowed me to open up the dusty book of my early memories and rediscover where these mysteries had first planted themselves in the soil of my unconscious. This was not, apparently, the first time I had encountered the arcane in the bright light of day or the dim shadows of night. Those long buried memories were the seeds that had slowly been growing in the dark fields of my hidden life. Their strivings for the light had finally provided the push that led me into the world of meditation.

The Way Forward

To fully comprehend where meditation had brought me and to what revelations it would subsequently lead, I needed to excavate those hidden memories. Only in this way could I understand the nature of the forces driving the genesis and evolution of my practice. This was important since the secrets that might be uncovered by meditation were not necessarily all benign. Peering through the lens of meditation had given me a glimpse of the clouds of unseen forces and energies swirling around me. But like the ancient explorers had said, "Here there be monsters." If these forces were exposed prematurely, before I had grown enough through my meditative practice to understand their roots and constructively assimilate them, they could become like the tide, lapping at the foundations of my so-called sanity.

Postscript

Before I leave this story, there is one critical question I feel must be asked, one that has only recently surfaced within my consciousness and haunts me as I write these additional words, two years to the day after having begun my meditative practice. It's strange that only now I have begun to have this kind of existential doubt. At the time it happened and when I first wrote this chapter no such doubt existed. But it's here now. Was writing this book to blame? If so, readers beware. But maybe you were already asking this same question on your own. That question is this:

"Which was the *hallucination* and which was *real*?
The woman or the dog?"

Whatever opinion you have already formed about this issue may very well change as you read further into this book. I hope to return to this question before I complete my account and find a way to successfully exorcise this doubt.

Fig. 5. The Frog Knows the Answer

2. The Initiation Experience

The Tale of the Trickster's Maze

The incident of the shaggy dog raised a lot of questions in my mind about where the practice of meditation had taken me and about the nature of the forces behind these experiences. As I pondered these issues, I was reminded of a traumatic event that occurred when I was a young boy, an event in which I had my first powerful confrontation with the unknown. This also occurred in the light of day, though under very different circumstances.

This event was key, for it set me inextricably on the spiritual path that after many decades ultimately lead to the journey described in these books. It was the moment when mysterious spiritual forces reached out from some unknown place and called me into their future service, cementing in me a hunger for knowledge that was to appear in so many different ways in my life.

I will present this event in the form of a fairy tale. I use the challenge it presented as a metaphor for the endeavor begun in my Practice and continued in this work. This short tale will be the only time when I must explicitly supplement materials from my memory with an imaginary narrative. All my other visionary accounts will be drawn entirely from actual experiences.

Although the basic events of this encounter were real, I am unable to recall the details of the conversation. All I remember was that some kind of conversation took place, one involving an apparition who called himself Death. The dialogue recounted here, therefore, is a reconstruction, probably more representative of the current state of my unconscious than that of the young protagonist in the story.

The Trickster's Maze

Once upon a time there was an introverted little boy about seven years old who was preoccupied with the mysteries of life. I was that boy. In my mind the world didn't fit together as well as everyone pretended it did, especially those grownups. It was a mystery why I was so dissatisfied with the many fables taught to children: was it genetics, was it karma? Could one be born a philosopher? Whatever the cause, I was full of questions. Thoughts were my most favored companions, however ill formed and shallow they might have been at such a young age.

Day after day, whenever I could find some quiet time, I thought and I thought, but no revelations came to me, only more questions. All I found were mysteries piled on more mysteries. I was, after all, just a little boy. I had neither the experiences nor the faculties needed for such an endeavor.

But one bright sunny afternoon when I was home sick with a high fever in my bedroom, something changed. A portal opened up before me, and a strange apparition appeared, perhaps conjured up by the silent summons of some wayward, unexpressed thought.

Sitting perched on top of the vertical chest of drawers directly across the room from me was a strange apparition about the size of a small child; it was about three feet tall, with legs casually dangling down the front. Though it was dressed all in black, it reminded me of some kind of misshapen leprechaun. Its appearance flickered in and out between two different kinds of entities, one time a diminutively sized elfish man, another time a frightening, spider-like beast.

Sometimes for arms and legs it had multiple thick hairy limbs that looked like the legs of a giant tarantula. Atop its body sat a bearded black-eyed face covered in grey fur and spiky dark hair. Other times it appeared as a grey-bearded old man with intense, penetrating dark eyes and animated outstretched arms. At times these arms seemed to be reaching out for me. It was impossible for me to focus on either of the shimmering shapes. My vision had become cloudy.

'Little boy, I come in answer to your summons. I bring answers to all of your questions. But prepare yourself. I am Death. Today I come for you. Join me and all will be made clear,' said the apparition, whom I will call the "Trickster." To entice me, he parted the veils between worlds and let me peek inside the crystal ball he carried.

'Stop it! Leave me alone!' I cried. I felt a force pulling me out of bed, which I resisted with all my fevered strength. I did want to know the Trickster's secrets but I did not want to die. And I was frightened by what I had glimpsed and the thought of what terrible truths the secrets might reveal.

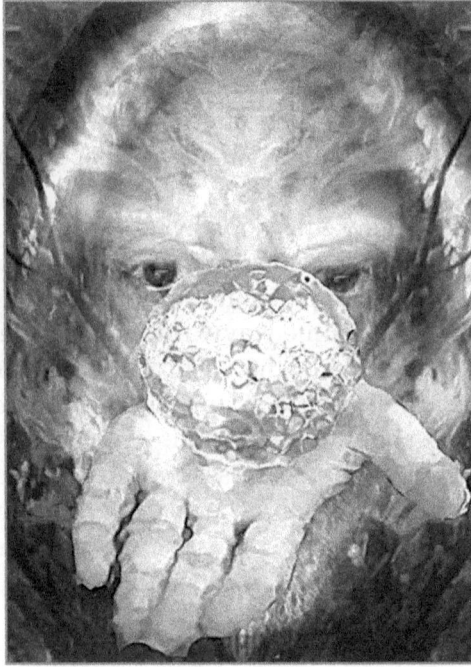

Fig. 6. 'Come with me now'

My will vacillated as I waged a battle both with the Trickster and between my own desires and fears. The tug of war went on for what felt like a long time but was probably only a few minutes, until finally the Trickster relented. I fell back exhausted onto my sweat soaked bed.

'Why do you resist?' asked the Trickster. 'Don't you want to know my secrets? Were you fooling yourself with your silly little riddles as you played at philosophy?' said the Trickster.

'Maybe this is just a game to you. But you've seen things forbidden to the living. You are now caught in my web. But all is not lost. There is a secret path through my web's maze that will bring you the freedom and the answers you seek, but only if you can find the right threads to follow. *That is the task I charge you with. You must find my treasure.*'

The Trickster explained the challenge confronting me. He said I would receive clues hidden in dreams and visions. My task was to decipher the meanings concealed within these experiences and uncover the secret guidance they provided. If I followed this guidance, my journey through the maze would lead to the promised reward.

'Wait,' I said, struggling to sit up, 'I know what dreams are. What's a vision?'

'Stupid boy,' he responded, 'what do you think this is?'

I blinked at him and shook my head, trying to focus my attention and see more clearly. None of this made any sense. What was happening to me?

'If you are done with your nonsense, I will continue.'

He said that additional clues would appear in my waking life, but only at the very edge of my awareness. The Trickster warned that counterfeit signs would also appear. If I let these fool me, I would be led astray. Like the fly in the spider's web, I would become more and more entangled in its threads.

Once I began the game, the Trickster said, I would forget this whole encounter. The game would be played out in my unconscious, at least until I had acquired enough clues to make me once again conscious of my quest.

'Now,' said the Trickster, 'it begins. Be careful in your choices. Find the threads. Follow the clues. The next time you awake, you'll be in my maze, but you'll soon forget all about it.'

'Oh, by the way,' he added. 'There is one final riddle you must solve before your task will be complete. You must identify me. You must find the answer to the simple question: "*Who am I?*"'

Commentary

Another Fractured Fairy Tale

This childhood memory came to me as I began to write these words, nine months to the day after I had first started sitting in meditation. Yes, it was a rather grim fairy tale about a young boy's confrontation with the unknown. In this tale, life, like the Trickster's Maze, was an obscure labyrinth with few paths leading to redemption and many more to disillusionment. But it also raised the possibility of an escape from this maze that could be found in the hidden patterns of meaning buried in dreams and visions. It offered the hope of liberation. And it marked my first initiation onto the mystic path.

Why had this story come to me now as I write these words? It made me wonder what other strange thoughts might be growing in me, ready to come to term. This story joined a series of other baffling visions and encounters I experienced since beginning meditation. But there was something special about this story. For it was more than just a fairy tale. It was a memory that meditation had retrieved from deep in my subconscious. Had I brought back something more than this splinter of memory from what was possibly a near-death experience? Had this memory shown me a way out of the Trickster's Maze by replaying this initiation experience?

I do know something strange and otherworldly occurred that day. Even though many of the details faded from my fevered memory days after the event, apparently I had described this event to my parents the day it happened. I learned this later in my childhood, when, much to my surprise, they repeated the tale of the Grim Reaper. They thought nothing of it, believing it to be simply the hallucinations of a sick child. I obviously felt the same way, having so successfully suppressed its memory for so long.

I know now that what I had seen that day was neither Death incarnate nor some kind of bizarre Spider creature, but rather an apparition sent by my Soul to initiate me onto her path, even as she hid her true identity behind these macabre disguises.

Practitioners from other traditions who are reading this account might suppose that I was visited by a spirit from another reality that day, one who sensed that I was starting to slip into its world. But I maintain that other reality is in fact located in the internal realms of my Soul, rather than within the realms of some other external dimension. As I was to learn, *these two realms really are the same thing*. Only our ways of speaking about them differed.

Not Easy Being Green

In spite of its strangeness, the Trickster's Maze concealed a potentially significant revelation. To discover what it was, I would ultimately have to solve the Trickster's final riddle. Fairy tale or not, I was caught in the metaphorical web spun by the tale of the Trickster and probably have been for much of my life. Having seriously begun meditating, following the discipline I call "the Practice," I needed to find my way out.

So there I was in Mission Plaza Park, one hundred and thirteen days into my journey. And here I am now as I begin to relate this story. It is September 27, 2014, exactly nine months since I began the Practice. This account will be meditation's real progeny. I have consciously taken up the challenge of the Trickster's Maze.

If I want to escape this maze, I must find the threads hidden in my visionary experiences. In the absence of recognizable landmarks, I need to create my own. Otherwise, I would be like a frog without his pond, or maybe, given where I find myself as I write these words, more like a tadpole trying to escape the murky waters. But that is my challenge.

The Way Forward

The good news is that I do have a collection of memories to plumb, both those recovered from a small set of enigmatic dreams, as well as those from my visionary travels. Each is a potential clue I can use to try to create a more coherent map of where the Practice was leading me, even as I continue to tell its tale.

It is time to spread out all the clues I've collected and see which ones I can fit together, chronicling the interwoven stream of visions that began the very first day of the Practice. To this mix I will also add material from several dreams experienced prior to the Practice that now seem important to understanding my story.

All told, these dreams and visions are like jumbled pieces of a jigsaw puzzle that tumbled out of a newly opened box onto the table. But this is a puzzle whose final solution would only be known when it was completed. There would be no handy picture provided for me on the box's cover. The *Tao-Te-Ching* spoke of an image that could guide me, but only if I could find it. As chapter 35 says,

> *"Hold in your hands the Great Image.*
> *All under Heaven will come to you.*
> *Their coming will not bring harm,*
> *But great tranquility and equanimity."*

With or without this image, in these pages the game of the Trickster's Maze will commence for real.

3. A New Approach to Vision Analysis

Developing a Method

Learning How to Listen

Confronted with the Trickster's challenge of the maze, I made the explicit decision to treat the visionary experiences obtained in the Practice as the coherent expression of hidden facets of my Self. If I viewed them instead as the illogical meanderings of a brain creating a narrative from random discharges, I would learn nothing from them. I would receive no new signs to point my way through the maze. My work will be guided by the assumption that visions are the best way for my unconscious Self to communicate with me. If my true Self spoke to me using the language of the Soul, I needed to learn how to listen.

A Comparative Anatomy of Visions

To navigate my way through the seemingly disparate panorama of symbols and experiences found in my meditative travels, I have developed a method for identifying the common motifs and patterns they contained. My approach borrowed from both Western and Eastern methods for analyzing our inner lives and the ways we experienced the world around us. Researching these various traditions enabled me to start making progress with what seemed a confusing tangle of experiences. The framework that emerged allowed me to ultimately identify the elusive narrative threads that would tie my visions together.

From the Western perspective my approach draws most heavily from the work of C.G. Jung, who described his project as developing a comparative anatomy of the psyche. Jung experienced a period of intense visionary encounters early in his career, and much of his later groundbreaking work was shaped by the revelations fueled by these visions. He wrote about these in a remarkable private work, *The Red Book* (Jung 2009), which remained unpublished for many years after his death. While dreams were ultimately his primary domain of study, mine will be focused on the visions that appeared during meditation. One of the goals of my work will be the creation of a "comparative anatomy of visions," similar to Jung,

Given the enigmatic nature of my visions, this type of approach is essential to my work's possibility of success. Whatever systems of rules or logic the world of the Soul possessed were ones I could only try to deduce *ex post facto*. This was the challenge presented by my visions as I struggled to find my way through the Trickster's Maze. These books will read like an extended mystery novel, as I endeavor to collect and decipher the meaning of the scattered visionary clues left me by my Soul. I hope what the Soul was telling me will become progressively clearer as this work continues.

The fact that I am writing these books while continuing the Practice means that I might be discussing visions that occurred on a day I was writing about earlier visions. This raises the possibility that my analysis and interpretation of earlier visions would influence the content of future ones. However, the vast majority of visions I will discuss occurred before I started writing and certainly before I tried to understand their implications. It was probably the heft of their unexplored mass weighing on my spirit that propelled me towards this endeavor.

Channeling the Active Imagination

The vision framework I propose is a key tool in the practice of what I call "metatation," the process of interpreting and reflecting upon meditative experiences. Sometimes the practice of metatation can take place within meditation. But an even more significant part can take place at a later time. The metatation approach brings my analysis more into line with Jung's comparative anatomy of the psyche.

Much of the legitimacy for this approach follows from my belief that the same forces that created meditative visions have the potential to productively guide post-meditational analysis, providing they are carefully channeled. Jung embraced these subliminal forces in developing his methodology and called his interpretative approach "active imagination." I recognize that achieving this kind of synchronicity between the vision and its analysis is difficult; its success can only be judged by the quality of its product. But I think that if my faith in the revelatory powers of the Soul is valid, the result of this approach will be a coherent and integrated narrative.

Given the kinds of flights of fancy that imagination might so easily degrade into, I maintain that any analysis built upon the foundation of active imagination needs to be guided and structured with a more rigorous methodological framework than post-Jungian psychologists typically employ. Only then will meditational exegesis have a chance of maintaining the integrity of the experience being investigated. This kind of integrity is critical for preserving the factual nature of the account, something I am committed to doing in this work.

Asking the Right Questions

In order to begin the process of uncovering the meanings and patterns hidden within my diverse visions, in this first book I will focus on different ways to look at the information content of visions, guided by the famous four *"W"* questions ("who" "what," "where," "when") journalists are trained to answer in the lead paragraph of a news story. Then, beginning in the second book of this series, I will supplement this approach with additional material introduced from Taoist philosophy and especially from the classic work, the *I Ching*, to document the process by which the nature of the Self may be uncovered through the characterization of the Soul's journey across the different realms of the mystical Worlds.

Regarding the "W" questions, the "who" question will focus on the characteristic identity of myself and the presence of other entities within the vision, the "what" on the qualities of the vision's content and expression (visions will not always be "visual"), the "where" on the realm in which the vision took place and the domain elements of the associated worldview, and the "when" on the nature of my state of consciousness when I experienced the vision. I will also address the "how" question by examining my role within the vision and the manner in which I experienced it. At this point I will not address further the question of "why" I am having these visions, since I've already made the working assumption that the Soul and its forces are driving their genesis.

As part of my "how" analysis I have identified five different types of consciousness: External, Threshold, I-Maginal, Deep Trance, and Dream. The middle three are the most relevant to the different types of meditational experiences. *Threshold* consciousness

18

is the relaxed state I attain initially during meditation. *I-Maginal* consciousness (to distinguish it from "imaginal" and what we normally think of as the imagination) is where I normally experience visions, and *Deep Trance* is a special state that is devoid of all but the most primitive form of awareness, a state not normally recoverable by other states of consciousness.

I have discovered that by analyzing my visions in terms of these questions, I was able to identify a series of distinctive motifs and thematic elements in my visions. I will use keywords to indicate these motifs, in order to categorize each vision. For each vision I will present the result of my analysis in a summary table called the "Vision Matrix." As I discuss my various visions, I will identify the motifs that apply to them and highlight what is most distinctive. When appropriate, I will also call attention to special issues raised by features of particular visions. In the Addendum to this chapter, I will include additional information on how to read the Vision Matrix.

Thematic Narratives

In addition to identifying common motifs that different visions share, this approach will also enable me to discern features of narrative or plot shared among a series of visions. These features allowed me to see the visions as part of an integrated and evolving storyline following the Soul's journey. I call this type of "inter-meditational" grouping a "thematic narrative." The distinctive location in which a series of visions occur (their "realm") will be key to identifying a vision's membership in a particular thematic narrative.

In my experience the content elements of a particular thematic narrative usually maintain a one-to-one relationship with a specific visionary realm. In other words, each realm is typically associated with one and only one narrative's content, and each narrative's content will take place entirely within a specific realm. This rule does not apply to the visions serving as transitional elements into or out of the realms associated with the content of the narrative. These visions function more as symbolic doorways into the narrative's realm rather than being part of the narrative's actual content. Syntactically, they act as the entry or exit components bracketing a narrative's base content.

Because of the expository power of the thematic narrative, I will use this concept in subsequent chapters as a way to organize the presentation of my visionary journeys. In most cases the experience of visions grouped in these narratives will occur sequentially in time, although other visions might be interspersed within this temporal sequence that were not included as part of that narrative.

In addition to grouping visions together based on shared thematic components, there is another special type of grouping that occurs entirely because of the way in which they were experienced. This is the case in which I experience multiple, distinct visions within a single meditative session. These visions are separated by interludes of non-visionary meditational experience. During these interludes I am able to reflect, however briefly, on the vision just experienced. Sometimes these clustered visions contained segments of an unfolding scenario that got interrupted. Other times these visions might be completely different in content or presentation.

I will refer to this way of grouping multiple visions as a "session cluster." While the majority of my visions were not part of session clusters, I have experienced clusters of as many as five separate visionary episodes. I assume as a general principle that visions occur within a session cluster because of some underlying narrative connection. These clusters will accordingly be another example of how visions come to be grouped within a thematic narrative.

What Dreams Had Come

In the two chapters following the addendum I will introduce the use of the Vision Matrix by applying it to a pair of iconoclastic dreams from my past that built on the mystical momentum begun by the visit of the Trickster. The first of these chronicles a series of nighttime visits by an unseen force that tormented me as a child over an extended period and led me to distrust the world around me. The second presents a dream that depicted a cosmically catastrophic event immediately followed by a thundering voice making a disturbing pronouncement, one that attacked the supporting foundations of my most basic beliefs at the time. Both of these dreams significantly undermined key components of my accepted vision of the world and accelerated my journey down the path that was ultimately to lead to the Practice.

Addendum

The Format of the Vision Matrix

Headers

Each chapter will have the following headers:

Chapter # followed by Vision #: and *Name of Vision, or*
Chapter # followed by Dream #: and *Name of Dream*

Narrative and Motifs Section

Thematic Narrative: Name of Vision, # of current vision out of total number of visions in narrative

Session Cluster: # of current vision out of total number in session cluster

Motif Elements: list of motif elements

"One or Many" Section

In the following categories, a **bold** font will indicate the presence of those elements. *One or many* elements may be selected from each set.

Subject:

Identity, Thinking, Myself, Embodied, Imbedded, Absent

Identity: *is there a sense of self*
Thinking: *are thoughts present?*
Myself: *is the identity my own?*
Embodied: *do I have a body during the vision?*
Imbedded: *do the vision elements surround my body?*
Absent: *are none of the above attributes present?*

Content:

Visual, Background, Depth, Animated, Navigated, Empty

Visual: *is the vision visual or not seen?*
Background: *is there a well-defined background?*
Depth: *does the vision suggest three-dimensional depth?*
Animated: *are elements within the vision moving?*
Navigated: *do I move into different areas of the vision?*
Empty: *are none of the above attributes present?*

Domain:

Air, Human, Etheric, Symbolic

I will describe these domain elements when they appear in the book.

"One from Each" Section

In the following categories, only *one* element from each listing may be selected. For special cases, I will explain the meaning of these different elements during their initial use. In most cases their meaning will follow from their usage. Only the element selected will appear in the listing.

World Level: Surface World, Under World, Upper World
World Realm: External, Formal, Celestial, Zero, Home, Forest, Jungle, Ocean, Subterranean, Cavern, Mountain, Valley, Desert
Participation Mode: Embodied Subject, Embodied Other, Embodied Witness, Disembodied Witness, Pure Witness, Luminous Witness, Pure Presence
Involvement Level: Passive, Engaged
Population Level: Populated, Solitary, Empty
Direction of Focus: Right, Left, Above, Below, Centered
Consciousness: External, Threshold, I-Maginal, Deep Trance, Dream

4. Dream 1: *The Night Demons*

Vision Matrix

Thematic Narrative: Night Shadows 1 of 3
Session Cluster: 1 of 1
Motif Elements: Retreat, Confrontation, & Monster

Subject: Identity, Thinking, Myself, Embodied, Imbedded
Content: Visual, Background, Depth, Animated, Navigated
Domain: Human

World Level: Surface World
World Realm: Home
Participation Mode: Embodied Subject
Involvement Level: Engaged
Population Level: Populated
Direction of Focus: N/A
Consciousness: Dream

"The Night Demons"

When I was a child, about ten or eleven years old, and a couple of years after my daylight encounter with the Trickster, I experienced an extended period of nightly visits from the phantasms of what were usually called "night terrors." A key component of these terrors surprisingly involved my sleeping position. In those days I always slept on my stomach. Why that was important will soon become clear.

The dream always began the same way. I would find myself wandering about the pleasant little suburban neighborhood of Sharon Heights where I grew up. This was in the small town of Sharon, Massachusetts, which, interestingly enough, was recently selected in 2013 by *Money Magazine* as the best small town in America in which to live. Sometimes I would find myself alone, other times I would be with other children.

Soon, in the distance, I would hear a repetitive, booming noise and the ground would begin to shake. Spielberg got it just right in the movie *Jurassic Park* when the T-Rex showed up for the first time. Maybe he had the same nightmares as a kid. The thumps were the footsteps of an approaching monster or giant. I'm sure any good Freudian psychologist would tell you this scenario was just the manifestation of a child's repressed fear of adults, since they would seem like all-powerful giants to children.

Hearing these sounds I would run and hide, usually going into a house I didn't recognize. I would hide in the closet or under a bed or in the basement. By this point I would always be alone. I remember wondering where everyone else had gone. Did they know a better place to hide? They must have, for the booming thumps would grow louder and louder and closer and closer. This was usually followed by the destruction and dismantling of the structure in which I was hiding.

No matter where I hid, the monster always found me. When this happened I would immediately wake up. The monster's intentions for me in the dream world remain a mystery. I never saw the monster or experienced what it intended. I just woke up.

Or did I? That was the question. Certainly under the circumstances waking up seemed the thing to do. Up until this point this account probably sounded very similar to common childhood nightmares. But the monster wasn't done with me yet. There I would be, lying on my stomach in my bed in my room, the real one, not the dream one. It would still be dark though my eyes would be open.

But as I groggily returned to waking consciousness, I would feel this excruciatingly intense pain drilling into the center of my lower back. It wasn't a constant pain. It instead had an irregular ragged pulse to it, similar to an electric current arcing into my spine at a 90-degree angle. There was no sound. It felt as if an unknown entity was discharging painful beams of jagged energy directly into my back. At the time I thought of this entity obliquely only as the "Monster," not wanting to afford it any more solidity or legitimacy by giving it a specific name.

At this point, I had three main options. First, I could do nothing. But then the drilling pain wouldn't stop. Many times I tried the experiment of lying there as long as I could, thinking the pain would eventually stop. But I always gave up before the pain did and chose one of the other two options. The second option was to reach behind my back and place my hand, palm up, over the site of the drilling. Initially, the drilling sensation would go through my hand as well but soon thereafter would stop. That worked pretty well. The third option was the best if I could muster the strength to roll over onto my back. That would immediately put an end to things, though I did feel residuals of pain after the drilling sensation had stopped.

"Why didn't you just go to sleep on your back?" you might ask. I tried that, but mysteriously always ended up on my stomach in time for the dream. The only good thing that came out of all of this was that the monster dreams did stop when I hit my teenage years. This occurred after my family had moved into a new house in a new neighborhood. Was it puberty or the new house that did the trick? While most sleep scientists would assert that the onset of puberty was the reason my sleep terrors stopped, in my case they stopped on my first night in the new house. I don't know why.

The problem was that until the nightmares stopped, I went to bed every night fearing the onset of the dream, knowing that once in the dream, no matter what I did, the monster would always find me. In the dreams I kept looking for new places to run or hide, at times even reflecting within the dream on previous escape attempts and trying to come up with new strategies. Though I always knew how futile my attempts at evasion would be, I never stopped trying. By the way, while I do sleep on my side now, I have learned from sleep monitoring that when I enter REM periods, I always roll onto my back. I don't know when that first started, but looking back, perhaps that was a prudent adaptation.

Commentary

To this day, I am still haunted by the newly retrieved memory of these dreams and the mystery of the painful drilling sensation that followed me into my waking state. The rationalist in me still believes the drilling sensation must have been a continuation of the dream state. I must have been in some undocumented shadow zone between dreams and waking. As a child I never told anyone about these troubling dreams, not wanting to add any potential new traumas to my life.

Sleep science identifies a spectrum of disorders that might be relevant to my experiences in this transition zone between sleeping and waking. Of particular relevance is a type of experience known as a "hypnagogic hallucination." People with this disorder remain awake in the mind but paralyzed in the body during the process of falling asleep or waking up. This kind of paralysis is due to the fact that during REM sleep, which refers to the rapid eye movement observed during dreaming, our body is normally paralyzed to protect us from self-injury. In hypnagogic hallucination, however, the brain is a little out of sync in its timing while initiating or removing the blockage. It either engages the blockage prematurely while the person is falling asleep or delays its removal after the person wakes up.

Night Terrors?

In some people these waking transitional experiences are so intense they are characterized as night terrors. Sleep labs have established that even though these patients indicated they were awake, their monitored brain waves showed they were still asleep. This observation is somewhat complicated by the fact that the brain waves that occur while dreaming exhibit the same kind of high-frequency waves found in a waking state. Still, my experiences certainly resembled this well-documented phenomenon of night terrors.

To help people experiencing night terrors, doctors have devised techniques designed to enable sufferers to escape from their sleep paralysis. Though paralyzed, they trained individuals to at least make some kind of minimal movement, such as rolling their eyes or wiggling their toes or fingers. The goal is to convince their brains that they are awake, thereby making it safe to remove the paralysis. In my case sleep doctors would probably have maintained that the act of moving my arm or rolling over would have been a strong enough signal to convince my brain that I was awake and no longer dreaming. That would have been their explanation for why the pain would have stopped.

This explanation doesn't work in my case though, since not only was I able to move my arms when I should have been in sleep paralysis, but, more significantly, the act of moving did not by itself end the experience. When the event was happening, rolling my body onto its side or moving my arm into a position not directly over the drilling location had no effect on terminating the dream or the accompanying sensation. As a budding pre-teenage scientist I tried those experiments. The act of willed bodily movement was not sufficient to stop the transmission of the dream-induced pain.

Only if the site of the sensation were actually covered, either by my hand or my back on the mattress, would the dream end and the pain sensation stop. Whether I was wearing pajamas or sleeping under many layers of blankets was irrelevant to the experience. Apparently, my mind was totally locked into the reality of the dream-induced sensation. Only an action that made logical sense within the dream's imagined narrative and was judged sufficient by its own standards of validity would sever the connection to the drilling current.

The upshot was that my so-called waking dreams as a child both had the ability to induce sensations of physical pain upon awakening and the power to enforce their own narrative. In this narrative pain could only be ended by specific kinds of ritualistic behaviors consistent with the imagined causal laws of that narrative. Leaving aside the issue of the pain, what was significant about this phenomenon was the ability of the dream world to bring its version of the rules of causality across the border between the dream world and the real world.

Dream logic had the ability on these occasions to supersede the normal rules of logic that applied in my world. Using the terminology of quantum physics, it was as if a superposition had occurred between two different worlds, the dream world and the physical world. This blending of the two had created a hybrid world in which the laws of each world competed for dominance. This blended world was precarious. As was the case in quantum physics, when the dream world was observed and manipulated by the senses of the physical world, it would collapse, much as meditative visions often did when attention was focused on them.

Keeping Me on the Path

Was there something positive I could glean from these waking nightmares of my childhood? That's clearly a tough challenge because they were a riddle for so much of my life. In fact, I believe that as a naïve child I had completely misunderstood the real meaning of the dream, as well as the import of the drilling sensations that always followed it. I had misread all the clues and, as the Trickster might have put it, grabbed all the wrong puzzle pieces. I believe now that rather than being some kind of demonic attack, it was instead another instance of a shamanic-like initiation experience, much like the visit of the Trickster had been.

The giant in my dream wasn't a monster or the personification of my fear of adults. It was instead the symbolic archetype of a being with seemingly godlike powers who sought me out in the state of my altered consciousness for a purpose known only to it, and maybe someday to me, but only when I was ready. It was my Soul projecting itself into my dreams as an unseen apparition, much like the one that had appeared a couple of years earlier as the ominous specter of the Trickster, both having been sent to keep me on the correct path.

This explains why I would always be found in my dreams, no matter where I would try to hide. You can't hide from your own internal gods and you can't run from your own Soul, not when the Trickster had spun its web throughout the reaches of your unconscious. You would always be caught. The roots of my fear went much deeper than a childhood fear of monsters. They lay in my fear of the unknown and in my refusal to accept the path my Soul had put me on. The fact I never saw this being or witnessed it causing any harm to anyone undermined the validity of my belief that it was malevolent. And that could be why I always awoke before I learned the true nature of the impending encounter. *I wasn't ready to confront the true face of the Soul.*

The Gate of Life

What about the painful drilling sensation that occurred when I came out of the dream? How would that fit into this scenario? The important thing to notice in this regard was that I always experienced the stream of energy going into me, rather than the other way around. In the classic folktales about the nighttime visitations of the vampire or succubus, the monster would always be draining energy from the victim, not putting energy into him, and usually from the region of the head. The fact electric-like energy was being given to me in my lower spinal area indicated that I was receiving an influx of new energy into my nervous system that would remain in reserve until its activation was needed.

The region where I received this energy, as seen from the front of my body, corresponded to what Taoists called the *"dan t'ian"* or "field of elixir." This was the area in which the *ch'i* or vital energy was accumulated and stored, the so-called *"sea of ch'i."* From the standpoint of my spine, the location where I received the energy also had an important acupuncture point located there, called the "*ming-men.*" This was a significant energy center described in the literature as the "gate of life" or the "gate of power," among other labels.

The reason the experience had felt so painful might have been because my channels for receiving this energy had not been opened yet. The energy would have had to bore its way through the obstructions that remained in me. The Chinese alchemists would say my gateways were blocked. The energy stream did allow me to terminate the flow when I could not tolerate receiving any more by a simple gesture of interrupting the beam with my hand or rolling over onto the bed. Had its source been actually malevolent, an actual demon, it could certainly have made things much more difficult to stop.

Who or what entity could have been supplying the energy in this scenario or what the purpose of this energy infusion was will have to remain a mystery for now. Instead of a demon I had my own energy daemon, where "*daemon*" in Greek mythology referred to entities that were benign nature spirits, portrayed there and in the shamanist traditions as spirit helpers and teachers.

These night terrors haunted me for much of my childhood and adolescence. Even after they stopped, for many years I feared the possibility of their return. They profoundly undermined my belief in the sanity and benevolence of the world I inhabited. I suspect one of the reasons I delayed the beginning of a real meditative practice for so long was due to my lingering fear about what I might discover lurking in the dark shadows of the Soul's hidden realms.

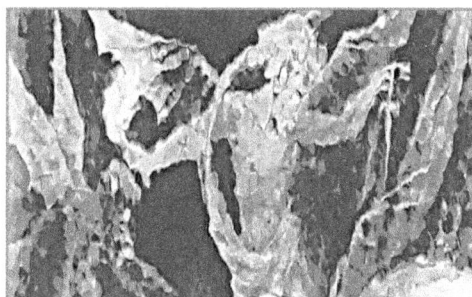

Fig. 7. Demons of the Night

5. Dream 2: *Cosmic Echoes*

Vision Matrix

Thematic Narrative: Night Shadows 2 of 3
Session Cluster: 1 of 1
Motif Elements: Dialogue, Vigil, & Gods

Subject: Absent
Content: Visual, Background, Depth, Animated
Domain: Air

World Level: Upper World
World Realm: Celestial
Participation Mode: Pure Witness
Involvement Level: Passive
Population Level: Empty
Direction of Focus: Centered
Consciousness: Dream

"Cosmic Echoes"

I had this dream when I was around fourteen years old, several years after the dreams of the "Night Demons" and six years after I had met the Trickster. The dream occurred in the early morning hours, around 2 or 3 a.m. Like any teenage boy, I should have been dreaming about girls that night, since that was pretty much what I would usually be thinking about every night when I went to sleep. But this night something was different. In this dream I had no body. I was just an incorporeal spot of awareness floating in a dark, vast, three-dimensional void.

The void was not empty for long though. It soon filled with stars and galaxies and comets and shooting stars. Yet there was not a sound to be heard. It was totally quiet but in an eerily foreboding way. I surveyed the wondrous scene before me as if I were seeing the Cosmos through the eyes of God (or at least through the eyes of Neil deGrasse Tyson). I had no sense of self or identity, nor did I engage in any thoughts as I witnessed the scene before me.

Apparently I was there only as a witness for what was about to transpire.

Suddenly there was a deafeningly loud blast of booming, reverberating sound, similar to what I had heard as a child when there was a lightning strike on the tree in my backyard. It sounded as if the heavens themselves were being torn apart. And, yes, in my dream they were. Simultaneously with the sound, a blinding, yellow-white flash of lightning occurred. It ripped its jagged way diagonally across the vast cosmic expanse spread out before me.

After the flash had subsided, a pulsing yellow crack remained, bisecting the panorama of the star field. Slowly, the tear became wider and wider. Inside the rift was a roiling mass of blinding white flames and balls of bright yellow and fiery red energy, churning and spitting inside a river of blazing plasma.

Fig. 8. The Big Rip

I heard a low roaring sound. Then, suddenly all sound ceased. For a moment there was dead silence. Then a thunderous voice spoke, as loudly as the initial explosion, saying without any inflection just these four words:

"THERE ... IS ... NO ... GOD."

These words reverberated across the heavens. Then I woke up.

Commentary

This is another one of those dreams I never told anyone about at the time, especially since I had no idea what it meant. I'm not sure I got much more sleep that night after I woke up because I spent hours trying to understand the implications of the strange anti-theological manifesto issued by this unknown voice. What did it mean and who or what was the speaker? In some ways it felt like the Cosmos itself was speaking to me and proclaiming its independence.

Was this actually my own declaration of independence from religious dogma, which I perhaps equated with the religion of my fathers, rather than the Universe's proclamation of freedom? Freud would probably have had something to say about that. At that point in my life I was not ready to engage in such psychoanalytic reflection. Instead, I tried to reason out the meaning of what I had just experienced. The internal dialectic I conducted went something like the following. My contemporary comments on this dialogue are in parentheses.

If there were no God, then who was it that was supposed to be speaking? It couldn't be the Devil, for you can't have the Devil without having God. Maybe it was the Devil and he was lying to me, trying to weaken my faith. But the Devil would know I would know you would need God to create the Devil, so that couldn't be it.

(I was starting to sound like the evil Vizzini in the movie *The Princess Bride*. No, I didn't really believe at the time this was some force from the unconscious speaking to me. But even if it was, the question would still remain as to what particular force it was and what was its agenda. To me the dream felt very real and troubling in its implications. Of course, believing what I do now, it may just have been the Trickster engaging in more shenanigans. At the time I was very much concerned about the existence of the Devil.)

And if there were no God, then who created the Universe? The voice didn't say God was dead or that God had somehow abandoned us after creating the Universe.

(I don't remember if I knew anything about Nietzsche back then, who famously proclaimed, "God is dead." The Time Magazine issue with the "Is God Dead?" cover didn't come out until 1966. This was 1963. The concept of God having abandoned us is now a common theme in many supernatural thrillers, in which warring angels fight for dominion over the scraps of a now abandoned Earth. Was it the voice of some renegade angel I had heard back then?)

Maybe the voice only meant a particular god didn't exist, specifically, the one I was raised to believe in. Or maybe the message meant there was no single God, but many gods as in the old polytheistic times.

(I was probably thinking of the ancient Greeks and Romans here. Even now, the concept of hierarchies of gods seems more plausible to me than just one single God. This approach did have the added benefit of providing me with a long list of potential candidates for the identity of the speaker in this dream.)

Simpler even still, maybe the message was that the concept of God as Creator was an unnecessary one. Maybe science could someday explain all of existence without needing to resort to God.

(Was I channeling the future Stephen Hawking here? At its foundations, you know, before the Big Bang, physical science seemed to me as faith-based as religion. And why would a random, materialistic, mathematically based universe need to provide me with such an ostentatious assertion of its independence from a Creator?)

Finally, maybe it all just meant the Universe was God and you didn't need a God in addition to the Universe. Maybe the Universe always existed in some form and didn't need to be created.

(I didn't have available to me the concept of an immanent versus transcendent god yet. I don't know if I knew anything about Buddhism then either. Prior to the Practice, this seemed to me the most plausible of all of the options listed here. However, even if true, why would the Universe have taken time out from its busy schedule to talk to me in this dream?)

As I recall, I didn't settle on any of these purported interpretations at the time, nor was I capable of any form of systematic, psychological self-analysis. Instead, I decided the question needed a lot more thought and study and then immediately forgot about it, leaving it to simmer in the unconscious. Questions about the existence and ultimate nature of God sporadically visited me for many years. This probably went a long way towards explaining my future interests in philosophy and belated plunge into meditation.

The Tao as Creator

Just as was the case for the "Night Demons" dream, I now understand this dream very differently because of what I have learned in the Practice. The real backdrop of the dream wasn't the Cosmos as I had assumed, but was instead the dream's symbolic portrayal of the internal realms of the Soul. The galaxies and stars seen in the dream do not just represent the ones existing in the external world. They also symbolize the many diverse worlds accessible to the Soul in its travels through the unconscious realms.

The vision's declaration of the non-existence of God accordingly has a very different meaning. It implies not only that there is no single being that is itself the creator and ruler of the worlds of the Soul, but also that the Soul itself is not a solitary, unified entity, self-created and self-existing. Something existed that was prior to it, something more primordial and fundamental, something like the Tao. As Lao Tzu says, speaking about the possible ancestry of the Tao in chapter 4,

> *"I don't know whose child it is.*
> *It appears to precede God."*

The rip in the universe indicated that behind the seemingly endless panorama of stars and galaxies, whether they existed in the external or internal Worlds, lurked a force much more primeval and boundless in its power. Much like the word of God was often shown emerging from pillars of flame, so too the voice of this force came out of the boiling cauldron of energy on which the universe floated like a crust. It did so to proclaim its dominion. The dream wasn't proclaiming the independence of the Cosmos. It was showing me that something else existed behind the Cosmos that

34

was much more powerful and ancient. It spoke to me not with the voice of God, but as the voice of the Tao.

Lao Tzu's chapter 4 describes some of these powers:

"The Tao rushes out and yet in its use
Nothing seems fuller.
So deep!
It seems the ancestor of the 10,000 things.
It blunts their sharpness.
It frees their tangles.
It softens their glare.
It is one with the mundane.
So profound!
It is as if it were alive.
I don't know whose child it is.
It appears to precede God (Di)."

According to various commentaries on this chapter, the ancient Chinese did believe in the existence of a creator they called "*Di*," who was viewed as the "Lord of Creation" and the supreme power. Lao Tzu is telling us in this passage that the Tao appears to be the ancestor of everything, including the God *Di*, much as I believe my dream was telling me as well.

6. The Philosophy and Methods of Meditation

My Philosophical Precursors

Following the Clues

My first real attempt at sitting in meditation was a long time in coming. I had made abortive attempts over thirty years ago. These were fueled by interests in Eastern spirituality and Chinese martial arts, which were themselves perhaps motivated by those episodes from my childhood (and yes, kung fu movies as well). But I lacked the necessary prerequisites of discipline, motivation, and patience even to make it through one short session. However, a lot can change in thirty years. On December 27, 2013 all the cosmic forces were aligned.

People begin meditating for a lot of different reasons and with many different expectations. On a conscious level I was especially interested in the philosophical aspects of meditation, since I had been researching different theories about consciousness and reality over the previous several years. I had followed a twisting path of clues about the nature of consciousness through the works of Western philosophers, cognitive psychologists, neuroscientists and physicists. Each of these provided new pieces of the puzzle.

Through these studies I discovered the philosopher Alfred North Whitehead, who in his famous work *Process and Reality* (Whitehead 1985) wrote that all reality was composed of droplets of experience synthesized in a process of free creation into new experiences. Each moment in the world was the collection of all the experiences that were occurring, which would then be replaced by a new moment with a new set of experiences that had evolved out of the combinations of the previous ones. For Whitehead, there were no subjects or objects in the world, no *things* populating reality. Instead, there were only *processes* involving experiences. Raw experiences and the processes that transformed them were all that ultimately existed in the so-called physical universe.

From there I was led to a series of writings on panpsychism, which held that everything that existed, even brute matter, contained an element of awareness and consciousness. This is different from saying that everything is alive. Rather, it assumed that everything had some degree of sentience. From the most primordial experience of force in the smallest subatomic particles, all the way up to the full-blown self-reflective awareness found in humans and possibly beyond, everything had their own distinctive, privileged view from within. A strong current of panpsychism flows through much of the history of Western philosophy, even though that fact has been successfully suppressed in traditional academic scholarship (Skrbina 2007).

Hierarchies and Emergence

The path of my investigations ultimately brought me to the integral philosophy of Ken Wilber and his opus *Sex, Ecology, Spirituality* (SES) (Wilber 2000). Wilber believed the universe (or "Kosmos" as he called it) was made up solely of nested holons, all the way up and all the way down, arranged in infinite levels of whole/parts, contexts within contexts, forever. Holons were not objects or processes, but a manifestation of a nested form of evolving consciousness.

Each level of holons represented the evolutionary growth of a new form of higher and broader consciousness. What was key to his concept of holons was that although each level was made up of those from the preceding level, it was more than just their union. It was something entirely new, driven by its own internal logic and principles, describable on its own terms, literally a new form of consciousness. Each level, as Wilber put it, included but transcended the previous ones. Wilber called his form of nested organization a "holarchy," intending to explicitly distinguish it from the more common concept of the hierarchy.

This kind of process of emergence is often characterized in terms of the creation of a whole that is "greater than the sum of its parts." I think this way of describing emergence can be somewhat misleading. Part of the difficulty stems from the fact that the components of the previous layers (the parts) contain entities that may no longer exist within the components defining the wholes at the higher levels. They would have been replaced by new kinds of entities. At some point in the process the component elements of the earlier layers have disappeared, so that the whole is a sum of *new* parts. How this all happens is where the mystery lies. Though we are all familiar with this general notion of emergence and its effects, we do not understand how it works. I would say, "We know it but do not understand it," to borrow an expression from Jung.

We know it, for example, as the hierarchical relationship existing between the different branches of science. The subatomic particles of quantum physics become the atoms and molecules of chemistry, which in turn become the larger objects, both living and inert, in the domains of biology and physics, and so on. You know the story: quarks become bosons and fermions, which become atoms, which become molecules, which a couple of stages later become Ken Wilber. We see that at each level there are now new kinds of objects, though at least in the physical sciences there is a sense that the new objects of the succeeding level are composed of those of the old. Here at least "parts is parts." It's the jumps between multiple levels that concern us.

While this type of scientific emergence is one we are fairly comfortable with, it is different from the type of emergence that occurs in the domain of conscious living entities. A better example for that is found in the concept of systems biology, which shows how networks of independent living components combine into networks of networks, ultimately resulting in the formation of the functioning living organism. Subcellular organelles interact with each other to help form cells; cells join together to form tissues; tissues work together to form organs; organs function together as organ systems; and organ systems cooperate to produce the overall organism.

What is significant about the systems biology example is that each component within the different interacting hierarchical levels is a living system, with its own type of worldview and laws governing its behavior, and if we subscribe to even a minimal form of panpsychism, its own form of consciousness and internal awareness. Even if we assume that rudimentary consciousness begins at the level of the individual living cell, this would mean that in the case of the individual human being, there would be roughly 37 *trillion* independent centers of consciousness, only 100 *billion* of which would be the neurons in our brains.

Until we know more about the processes that actually generate self-consciousness, the nature of the relationship that exists between the unified self-conscious of our mind and the 100 billion neurons within the brain and nervous system will have to remain a mystery. The biological entities that compose our minds us exist in worlds completely separate and independent from our own conscious lives. These worlds would be completely incomprehensible to us even if we could somehow obtain glimpses into their domains. The nature of the spiritual entities that compose our psychic lives is a whole different question, and one that these books are ultimately about.

Higher Stages of Awareness

Although Wilber has a complex four-quadrant theory looking at the parallel stages of conscious growth, the most relevant to the subject matter of this work is the Intention quadrant. Its stages range from the lowest level of prehension, representing the form an atom's awareness would take (following Whitehead) all the way up to what he calls vision-logic, which he views as the highest stage of cognition, a form of what he calls network-logic.

For Wilber, though, vision-logic was not the highest stage, but only the first one to move past rational thinking. Above it was a higher progression he called the "transpersonal," which traversed the different realms experienced by mystics following a contemplative path. As you would expect given Wilber's holarchical approach, he described four general stages of transpersonal development: the psychic, the subtle, the causal, and the non-dual. Since each stage completely transcended the preceding one, this progression was a very good example of the special nature of human consciousness.

The following is a quick summary of Wilber's transpersonal levels described in chapter 8 of SES, "The Depths of the Divine." I will be using these levels as part of my interpretation for one of the more complex thematic narratives I will encounter, the "Spirit Alchemy" narrative (in the next book). The reader is referred to Wilber's chapter for more details on these different levels beyond the synopsis given here.

- At the *psychic* level (p. 287), there is a direct experience of a universal Self or Soul, common to all beings. Wilber uses Emerson and Nature mysticism as examples of this level.

- At the *subtle* level (p. 301), there is a union of Soul and God, one prior to creation and its manifestation within the natural world. He calls this level Deity mysticism and illustrates it with writings from Saint Teresa.

- In the *causal* level (p. 309), Soul and God are transcended and dissolved into the realm of pure Self as pure Spirit. Wilber describes this level in terms of the Godhead or what Eckhart calls "God beyond God." He introduces Sri Ramana Maharshi's concept of the "I-I," which was how Ramana referred to the Self.

- At the final *non-dual* level (p. 317) the world of created Form and the Formless are no longer seen as two things but as one, in which, as Ramana puts it, the object to be witnessed and the *Witness* merge together into a unified Absolute consciousness. Here God is in all things and all things are in God. Wilber refers to this using Ramana's concept of the "I-I," calling it the "box the universe comes in."

What impressed me about Wilber's discussion of higher consciousness wasn't simply the breadth of his vision or the range of his scholarship. Rather, I recognized something in his writings that distinguished him from the vast majority of Western philosophers who wrote about consciousness and spirituality. He had undertaken the same internal journey as the spiritual masters he discussed. In contrast to most Western scholars, he believed you could never understand the message of the great sages unless you first shared in their experiences. I was taken by the authenticity I felt was present in Wilber's pursuit. But I still had questions about the genesis of his ideas, especially those concerning the transpersonal realms.

Had Wilber himself personally experienced these transpersonal stages in his meditation Practice? Or had he instead recognized qualities of these new levels of consciousness in the writings of the sages he assigns to each of these four transpersonal levels? Perhaps his own spiritual teachers had told him about them. Were these levels ones all practitioners would pass through once they attained suitable levels of transcendent consciousness? If so, would they experience them in the same ways or would their experiences be shaped and mediated by their cultural backgrounds? I don't know the answer to these questions.

What's Left Unsaid

In spite of this sincerity, I was left still wanting more by his descriptions of his own spiritual experiences. Although an articulate and precise writer, many of his personal accounts seemed to resort to the same type of New Age language seen so often in Western accounts of mystical experiences. Had his own spiritual teachers sworn him to doctrinal secrecy to protect the sanctity of the mystical realms in which they travelled? Where was the account of his experiential journey through these different stages? Many of the great sages had written about their own personal experiences as they traveled through these different stages of higher consciousness. Wilber discussed several of these in SES chapter 8.

Surely there must be more that can be said about the meditative journey beyond such commonly heard expressions as "I felt one with everything" or "All was illuminated" or "There was only Emptiness" or the Zen "Just *this*." Yes, the transcendent, revelatory experiences those expressions referred to were probably indescribable, as Wilber pointed out. But if there existed a series of staged visionary experiences that occurred along the way to the attainment of these more revelatory states, perhaps something more meaningful and descriptive could be said about them, especially if the transpersonal levels described by Wilber were real.

It was of course possible my suspicions were completely wrong. Maybe all visionary experience was so ineffable and deliciously alien in nature that only the kinds of inspirational accounts found in New Age culture were understandable for the Western audience. Perhaps that was why so many writers resorted to them. Or it could be, as many Zen schools held, that there was no set of stages one passed through on the way to revelation, no kind of journey. If it happened, it would just one day happen, suddenly.

I realized that in order to make progress in my studies and get to the bottom of the genuine mystical experience, simply reading the accounts of others, no matter how well written or evocative they might be, would just not do. If there were such a thing as a genuine spiritual journey, I would have to put myself on its path and walk its steps. To do so, I would have to overcome my own inhibitions about meditation and finally take the plunge for real. Then and only then would I discover the truth of what could really be said about the hidden realms of the spiritual world and what, as Wittgenstein said in a burst of mystical insight, *"Whereof one cannot speak, thereof one must be silent."* (Wittgenstein 1998, p. 108).

Taoism: The Road that Cannot Be Named

During this same period, I had been leading a small study group on the *Tao-Te-Ching* ("The Classic of the Way and its Attainment") by the ancient Chinese sage Lao Tzu. This work had always been important to me, and this was not the first time I had returned to it. The group was working through the original Chinese characters and comparing different English translations in order to try to understand better the subtleties of this enigmatic work. I soon came to see the passages concealed multiple layers of meaning. At the deepest level the work hid esoteric insights about the practice and experiences of Taoist meditative yoga. This revelation energized me. I later learned Wilber had been started on his own spiritual quest when he first discovered the *Tao-Te-Ching* in college.

The first chapter of the *Tao-Te-Ching* lays out the challenges and mysteries facing the spiritual seeker. This is my loose rendering from the original Chinese:

"The road to the Eternal cannot be walked.
Its name can never be spoken.
The Unnamed is the source of Heaven and Earth,
The Named things born from the Unbroken.
No-Desire can find the secrets hidden.
Desire knows only manifestation.
Hidden and manifest received different names,
But as one sprung forth from creation.
Their Union truly a mystery called,
Beyond where all mysteries hover.
For hidden deep inside we find
The doorway to the secret Mother."

As later chapters in the *Tao-Te-Ching* reveal in its idiosyncratically oblique way, only through meditation can the seeker begin to penetrate the mysteries spoken of in this passage.

To give a sense of the challenges involved in translating the original text, the often quoted first line of this chapter reads in Chinese: "*tao k'o tao fei ch'ang tao.*" The character "*tao,*" which is normally translated as "the Way," also means "road" or "path." As a verb it can mean "to follow" or "to describe," among other things. The character *"ch'ang"* has been translated as "constant," "standard" and "unchanging," as well as "eternal". A more literal translation of the first line reads, "Tao permitting Tao-ing opposed eternal Tao."

While much of the meaning of this chapter's verse is obscure, it does convey the message that thought and words alone will not provide access to the secrets of the Eternal Way (*ch'ang tao*). It points to the existence of a hidden Unity behind our surface world of desires and names that can only be found through a special form of experience. Was this the treasure I sought? Was this Way the way to the Self?

The Experience of Unity

Normal experience requires three separate types of entities: the subject who has the experience, the experience, and the identification of the thing experienced. For example, the "I am seeing a computer screen" has three separate components: the "I", the visual experience of seeing, and the recognition of the experience containing a computer screen. On the other hand, what about: "I am feeling sleepy?" Doesn't that have only two components: the "I" and the experience of sleepiness? Not really. Once again, we still have three: the "I", the experience of a particular physical sensation, and the identification of that sensation as "sleepiness."

The Unity hinted at in the *Tao-Te-Ching* could never be experienced this way, for there cannot be one when there were already at least three. The only way Unity could be experienced would be through a self-recognition of identity, or in other words, through a union of the experience with itself. It would be an experience of "I Am this Unity."

This is perhaps what Wilber meant when he talked about the non-dual or the "I-I". I understand Wilber's use of the "I-I" construction in the same way as I do the wording at the beginning of the first line of chapter 1 of the *Tao-Te-Ching*, where Tao is spoken of as "Tao-ing," as a subject-participle construction. This would mean that this state of consciousness was the one in which we experienced the "I" as "I-ing" and nothing more. A better way to express the unity of this state might be to describe it as just pure "I-ing".

In general, much of the confusion around the concept of "I" could be removed if we always understood it in discussions about states of self-consciousness as a verb, as in "to I," and never as a noun, "the I." This is to be distinguished from the common use of "I" as a subject, where it is simply a placeholder for the concept "self" or "persona." Self-identity then would be a case of "self I-ing."

When Words Fail

Trying to convey this experience of unity in words is difficult. The *Tao-Te-Ching* tells us it is impossible. We know words cannot always successfully describe new kinds of experiences. Suppose you read a scintillating account about a fabulous newly discovered species of fruit. This fruit contained combinations of flavors never before experienced. Could those words convey to you anything more than the palest hint of what awaited you? Probably all they could really successfully convey was the basic admonition, "It's really good. You should try it." Ironically enough, this latter admonition is probably the best reason you can give someone for why they should start meditation.

Only when you bit into the fruit and savored the new explosions of flavors could you begin to appreciate the uniqueness of the fruit's offerings or the eloquence of the writer's description. This is why the account of a beautiful sunset could only resonate for you if you had previously experienced the kinds of radiant, translucent colors it expressed. Or more fundamentally why you could never describe a shade of the color 'blue' to someone who had never seen color.

If words are so inadequate for everyday sensory experiences, how much more inadequate must they be for the ineffable experiences of the spiritual realm pointed at by the *Tao-Te-Ching*? The transcendent hovers far outside the scope of our normal experience. No words, no matter how poetic, will ever convey anything of its real flavor without your having tasted it before. Only then will the right words trigger recognition. "Oh yes, the 'Valley Spirit.' I know what Lao Tzu means by that in chapter 6. I'll never forget the feeling of that hollowness echoing right through me, vibrating my very soul."

I too wanted the taste of that experience. Wouldn't you? But how do you pursue an experience, as the first chapter of the *Tao-Te-Ching* warns, that can never be attained by anyone who desired it, precisely because of the very nature of the thing pursued? That is the riddle that echoes throughout the text of the *Tao-Te-Ching*. I try to capture the challenge posed by this riddle in the following verse. This is my attempt at distillation of its message:

> *You can always obtain what you most desire,*
> *But only if you don't want it.*
> *You can always find what you most seek,*
> *But only if you don't look for it.*
> *Only by acting can you obtain your goals.*
> *But you'll only succeed by doing nothing.*
> *The answers to all mysteries lie right before you,*
> *But the truth lies in the question, not the answer.*

These riddles are the kinds of clues contained throughout the *Tao-Te-Ching*. In later chapters Lao Tzu provided the outline of a method, a Taoist yoga, for solving these riddles. But he concealed this method behind poetic and figurative language. He always left the finding of the solution to the reader. He told of a secret doorway behind which was hidden the treasure so many sought; but he presented no map that could be followed. There was no map. The only path to the treasure is the one you crafted yourself by walking it.

All is not lost though. The *Tao-Te-Ching* does describe the type of lantern you need to light your way through the Tao and find the small crumbs left there for you to follow. That lantern is the Practice. As the Lao Tzu said in chapter 52, "*Seeing the small is called enlightenment… He who uses the light will come back enlightened.*"

My Approach to the Practice

Preparing for Meditation

The journey hinted at in the *Tao-Te-Ching* is a difficult and challenging one. The Practice promised no quick results. Accounts of meditation I read spoke of years or even decades of diligent practice that must pass before any genuine realization would occur, if ever. That is why this spiritual quest requires such a dedicated commitment at the onset if it is to have any change of success.

But being psychologically prepared is not sufficient. The Practice also imposes a physical burden on the new practitioner.

The spiritual discipline of yoga, whose name, according to many accounts, meant "union," has associated with it a strenuous regime of physical postures (*asanas*) and breathing techniques (*pranayama*). Another more literal translation is "yoke," implying that one must first learn to subjugate the body to make spiritual progress.

Similarly, the Chinese monks at the Shaolin Temple learned kung fu martial arts and energy cultivation skills called "*ch'i kung*" ("breath work") in order to give them the stamina for extended periods of meditation. The Indian Buddhist monk Bodhidharma, after he had himself spent nine years in a cave gazing at a wall, reportedly brought many of these techniques to Shaolin.

While I had conditioned myself physically, having practiced Chinese martial arts for many years, a major barrier to my beginning meditation still remained. This was the often-quoted requirement that sitting meditation must be performed in a full or half lotus position. Those kinds of positions were simply not attainable by me. While investigating the local Santa Cruz Zen Center, however, I discovered that their practice included the option of performing sitting meditation in a chair. The main requirement was that the back be kept upright and relaxed. That resolved my final issue. I was ready to begin my yoga.

My Method for the Practice

My plan for beginning meditation was as follows. I would sit in a soft, overstuffed leather green chair in an upstairs bedroom with the windows blocked to seal out as much light as possible. A test sitting in the chair revealed I would need better back support to maintain an upright posture. To address this issue I placed a round black Zen meditation cushion called a "*zafu*" against the back of the chair. That worked.

To help dampen the impact of background noise I played ambient "New Age" music downstairs and closed the bedroom door. Initially I used a station playing ambient music from an Internet radio station. Later in the Practice, after a couple of months or so, I started to employ various collections of mp3 recordings containing binaural beats designed to help induce meditational states through a process called "brain entrainment." This use of a rhythmic background to support meditative states produced effects similar to those elicited by shamanic drumming.

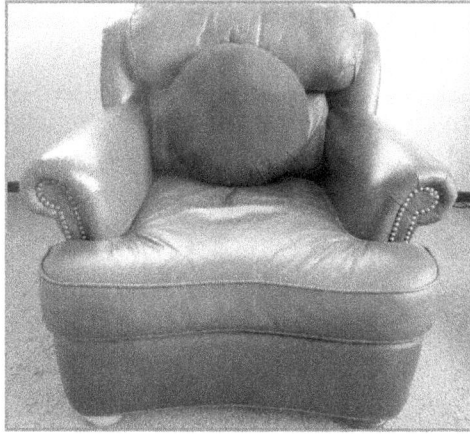

Fig. 9. My Chariot Awaits

I had hoped to sit thirty minutes that first day, so I had set a timer outside the room to let me know when my time was up. That way I would have one less concern to possibly distract me. Given my previous attempts, I had low expectations about whether I could even sit still for thirty minutes without an outbreak of serious fidgeting or ennui. But there I was that morning around eight a.m. lowering myself into my chosen chariot.

I rested my forearms on my upper thighs between the armrests of the chair. My hands were cupped with my palms facing upwards and thumbs touching. After some experimentation, I found a particular hand formation that seemed comfortable to me, in which the middle two fingers of the right hand where placed between the outer two fingers of the left before the hand was cupped. My feet rested on the floor, knees comfortably bent a little past the perpendicular. My upper legs slightly splayed out from the hips in order to support my forearms.

I learned later that this particular way of holding my hands together, one I discovered almost by accident, would prove critical to the process of opening up powerful channels of internal energy circulation in my body, as were other aspects of the way I placed my forearms on my thighs and rested my feet on the floor. As I've learned in my martial arts training, sometimes the smallest adjustments can make the greatest difference.

Following Taoist practice I let my eyelids fall until they were closed. I relaxed my jaw and placed the tip of my tongue lightly on my upper palate. This was also important for enabling internal energies to circulate in an unbroken fashion. In order to focus my mind I placed my internal attention on the swirling forms in the darkness behind my eyelids. Remembering Bodhidharma, I imagined my darkened room was my cave and the inside of my eyelids my wall. I began breathing slowly and softly through my nose and let all the tension drain from my body. The breaths were initiated from my abdomen rather than my chest. With that first breath my journey had begun.

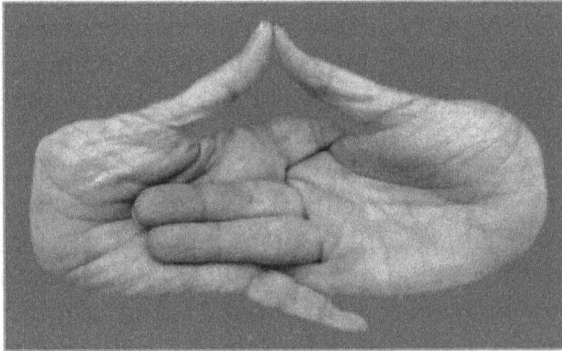

Fig. 10. The Secret Handshake,
"Hold in your hands the Great Image"

The Initiation Narrative: The First Door

The Guru, early testing and recruitment by the Watchers,
Followed by the appearance of the first door:
Tunneling towards the light

7. Vision 1: *The Ghost Guru*

Vision Matrix

Thematic Narrative: Initiation 1 of 5
Session Cluster: 1 of 2
Motif Elements: Entry, Visage, & Facsimile

Subject: Identity, Thinking, Myself
Content: Visual
Domain: Human

World Level: Surface World
World Realm: Formal
Participation Mode: Disembodied Witness
Involvement Level: Passive
Population Level: Empty
Direction of Focus: Centered
Consciousness: I-Maginal

Day 1: "The Ghost Guru"

Time slowly drifted by as I focused on the amorphous dark shapes floating across my visual field. I was surprised the background field was not solid. Instead it was somewhat pixelated with random patterns of grainy textures fading in and out of each other. The visual field was seemingly arrayed as a grid. Everything was dark. Some areas were a little brighter than others. Certain regions even had purplish blue hues. The shapes were constantly in motion and continually morphing in and out of quickly changing formations.

My breathing became very slow and shallow. I barely felt the air moving in and out. My body felt as if it had become part of the chair. I was still having occasional thoughts, but they seemed faint and very distant. I remember thinking this was fairly pleasant. The ambient sounds drifted away further and further into the background. My awareness seemed to contract.

Suddenly without warning I found myself somewhere else. All sound had ceased. My body was gone. If I was anything, I was pure spirit. I still had a sense of who I was, even as I felt myself immersed in a solid inky darkness devoid of any texture or variation. But I was not alone in this darkness. Suspended before me in the blackness was an old fashioned black and white photograph of a young man's head, which looked something like the following reconstruction (created when I wrote this chapter):

Fig. 11. Portrait of a Young Man

It reminded me of the headshots they used to take of us in school. Try as I might, I couldn't recognize the identity of the person in the photo. It was clearly not a picture of me as a boy. The person in the picture had dark features, but I could not place the nationality. Why was I seeing this picture? What did it mean? Thinking these thoughts was all it took to bounce me out of this realm and back into my room. I was still sitting in the chair with closed eyes.

In spite of the strangeness of this experience I was intent on continuing with the session. Everything felt as it had before this odd detour had occurred. The music played softly in the background. I resumed my focus on the dark shapes in my visual field and continued my steady, quiet breathing. The thoughts surrounding the mysterious photo slowly faded and were soon gone from my awareness. What I took to be the normal state of meditation resumed.

Commentary

Later that day I pondered the meaning of what I had seen (the vision of the "Ghost Guru"). I was more concerned with the question of its significance than the why of its sudden appearance. A black and white photograph had magically materialized before me, suspended in an inky black void, all within mere minutes of beginning my first meditation.

But why did it appear in black and white? We live in an age of high bandwidth media in which we are constantly bombarded by moving images in ultra-high resolution. We spend long periods of time staring at glowing computer screens. Yet my first vision had taken a decidedly low bandwidth route to deliver its message, using a still photograph. The image was not just in black and white; it was printed on what appeared to be old-fashioned photo paper, something almost extinct in this age of digital photography.

The obvious question was, "Why just a photograph?" Whatever imaginative faculty was doing all the work here could certainly have done better than a simple photograph. This is a "more is better" type of situation, especially if it was intended to shock me out of my self-imposed cosmic lethargy. At least give me a full-bodied 3-D animated phantasm. Give me what you got in the original *Star Wars* movie, when the Princess Leia hologram pops out of the robot R2D2 and says, "*Help me Obi Wan. You're our only hope.*"

I considered a possible explanation for why my first vision was not something more robust. Since I was brand new to meditation when the photo appeared, literally only about ten minutes or so into my meditation, my internal faculties were not yet developed enough to manifest anything beyond a photograph. I was, after all, just learning how to see in this new and potentially alien realm. The doorway to the secret realm of the Tao had just started to open. Perhaps the simple photo came through first to help orient me to this new domain. I did know, as I pondered these issues, that another more robust vision had come later in that same session.

Even if there were some truth to this, I still believed that the way the photo was presented to me was as much a clue about the identity of the subject as the actual image of the face was. Perhaps the presentation of the photo indicated the subject was someone who lived in a period when only black and white photos were possible. Or maybe the subject, since he appeared a teenager, grew up in the time before color photos became more common, as had been the case when I was growing up.

This interpretation, while plausible, raised an interesting question. I did not believe myself to be a character in someone else's mystery novel. At least, when I had this experience I didn't. Much, of course, has changed since then. One of the most important things I have learned is that *we are all just characters in our own mystery novel*. Yet, even then, at the very beginning of my Practice, I was apparently willing, however briefly, to consider the possibility that one part of my mind was presenting me with clues to a mystery that it wanted me, via another part of my mind, to solve. In spite of the prescient nature of that thought, it was not one I was prepared to seriously explore.

I considered that the most likely scenario was that I had seen a facsimile of this photo sometime in my past, perhaps in a book about a historical spiritual figure. I spent several weeks flipping through books I owned in search of this image. That search proved futile. The other possibility, of course, was this was an image I would see again in the future, having been alerted in advance to its significance by the vision. But though I wasn't ready to consider that possibility at the time, that attitude would soon change.

Mystery Solved? The Ghost Guru

The mystery of the identity of the individual in the photo was, in fact, solved several months later (at least to my semi-satisfaction). Three weeks after commencing the Practice I began reading works by the 20th century Hindu philosopher and mystic Sri Aurobindo. Aurobindo created a form of yoga he called "Integral Yoga," which some suggested influenced Wilber in his vision for an integral philosophy. Sometime later while reading the book *Beyond Man* (Van Vrekhem 2007) on the life and work of Aurobindo, I stumbled across a photo plate showing the young Aurobindo. It looked remarkably like a younger version of the individual I had seen in my vision. If my recollection was accurate, was this a case of the Practice activating a capacity for precognition or something more significant?

I considered some different possibilities regarding the significance of my having seen the image of the young Hindu sage. Had the spirit of Aurobindo come to welcome me at the beginning of my spiritual quest? There is an old saying in mystic circles that your guru appears in your life when you are ready. This appearance could take many forms, ones not necessarily embodied in the flesh. In particular, several traditions spoke of the possibility of encountering a "ghost guru." Gandhi, for example, wrote about his own experiences with such a being. Had the spirit of Aurobindo appeared to serve a similar role for me?

Several weeks after this vision and before I recognized the identity of the figure in the photo, I became an avid student of Aurobindo's writings and philosophies, and in particular his philosophical opus *The Life Divine* (Aurobindo 2010). This study continued for many months, through the most prolific periods of my visionary encounters. Certain of these spiritual experiences mirrored those described by him and his followers, especially the strange reverse Kundalini event of "The Awakening," while others led me off in other philosophical directions.

I still find his ideas about the integral nature of spiritual knowledge highly resonant with my own experiences. He believed there was an element of truth in all the different spiritual traditions, something I have seen first hand. I believe much of the symbolism in my visions does reflect elements of Aurobindo's teachings, but also those of Jungian depth psychology and classical Taoist alchemy. Other experiences are very similar to those described in Harner's work on modern shamanic doctrine (Harner 2013) and, of course, Buddhism. Some even resonated with passages from the *Gospel of Thomas*.

I did not discover the works of Jung or Harner until some time after the visionary experiences I will describe in these books had ended, however. That raises an interesting question. Were the integral correspondences with these theories that I found in my visions a validation of the shared nature of visionary experiences across different traditions, part of the so-called "perennial philosophy" (Huxley 2009)? Or were they instead instances of psychic foresight, since my Soul knew what works I would be studying in the future, maybe even because it would be directing me to them via its visions?

It is quite possible that Aurobindo's image in my first vision was a form of directed foreshadowing rather than an announcement of his guruship, the result of a subtle prodding by unconscious forces intent on leading me towards his writings. But maybe that just is what modern guruship looks like. Who was I to assume that I knew how my Soul would start a neophyte such as myself on my spiritual path? Maybe in the modern age of the Internet, with its easy access to sacred texts, the process of guruship takes on a very different form than the days in which it required the appearance of teaching spirits.

Aurobindo's image also conveyed another kind of allegorical message. The photo showed him as a young man. This was before he was to have his own mystical awakening and begin his long visionary odyssey, which he was to relate in fictionalized form in his epic spiritual poem, *Savitri* (Aurobindo 1995). Perhaps this was the metaphorical meaning I was meant to discover, that I was about to begin my own visionary odyssey and was destined to record it. I can only hope the much less poetic nature of my work will allow me to complete it in less than the 25 years Aurobindo devoted to his.

If this image of the mystic as a young man was a metaphorical "Before" picture depicting my neophyte status at the beginning of my quest, the reader can justifiably wonder if I will receive a visionary "After" picture at the end of the spiritual journey depicted in these books. Would I be shown an image of the prototypical Jungian archetype of the "wise old man" or would that final image be something completely different and unexpected? Unwilling to give away too much at this point, I can only offer the reader a qualified "yes" to both.

The Visage Motif

One of the predominant features of this vision was its presentation of an individual's face and head, the defining characteristic of the Visage motif. Sometimes, as in the present case, this motif takes the form of a two-dimensional image, while in others the head and face are rendered in a more realistic three-dimensional form, in both cases against a non-descript background. The image in this motif will always be static and unmoving, as would I. The face would look directly at me. I would see this face while I was in the form of a non-physical kind of being called a "Disembodied Witness."

While other visions I will discuss also involved images floating against a featureless background, the concept of the Visage motif is distinctive. I saw human faces floating before me many times in my visions. Of special significance is the series of different faces that appear to signal the approach of the final stage of my visionary journey. One of my challenges as this account develops is trying to understand the meaning and significance of the many different faces that materialized before me. The appearance of Aurobindo's image at the very beginning of the Practice foreshadowed the important role images of faces played in my journeys.

The Formal Realm

In most cases characterizing the location of a vision is fairly straightforward. For example, the location of my second vision was in the room in which I meditate, which is within the Home realm. But this first vision was somewhat unexpected and idiosyncratic in its presentation. It is not surprising, then, that this vision's location would need to be characterized in a somewhat unique fashion. But what type of location could be ascribed to the floating photograph, if its background environment was a featureless black void? This is where the concept of the Formal realm comes in.

I've included the general concept of realms within the Vision Matrix because it is a useful property for grouping specific sets of related visions together to form thematic narratives. The Formal realm in particular is important even though it is not the type of realm in which the base content of a thematic narrative usually appears. It does, however, often act as a syntactic marker designating the beginning and/or ending of these narratives. In this role it functions like the indentation at the beginning of a new paragraph, or the blank space following the last sentence at the end of that paragraph. It marks a point of entry or demarcation.

Unlike more substantial kinds of realms, the Formal realm represents the more abstract worlds of ideas and symbols. These generally appear in visions as allegorical imagery or symbolic constructs rather than as thoughts. The Formal realm is the closest analogue to the Platonic "world of forms" within my visionary experience. The facsimile of the human face appearing in this vision is an example of this kind of form.

The types of visual content appearing within this realm are typically objects and shapes from the domain of human experience.

These include visual symbols such as the photograph, for example. These forms represent the attempt by the Soul to find an accessible, non-verbal representation for certain types of meaning disclosed within visions. This particular type of realm is not restricted to the Visage motif. We shall see other types of motifs where it applies, usually at the beginning or end of the thematic narrative.

It is significant that this image from the Formal realm appears both at the beginning of this thematic narrative and at the start of my meditational Practice, signaling to me that the world is a much larger and stranger place than I previously thought. Whatever else I might say about this vision, it was as vivid and real to me as any previous experience. It announced to me in no uncertain terms the existence of a completely new type of realm, welcoming me into a brave new world. But my Soul was apparently not quite done with me that day, for it still had more surprises in store as my session continued.

8. Vision 2: *The Sitting Watchers*

Vision Matrix

Thematic Narrative: Initiation 2 of 5
Session Cluster: 2 of 2
Motif Elements: Vignette, Dialogue, & Vigil

Subject: Identity, Thinking, Myself, Embodied
Content: Visual, Background, Depth
Domain: Human

World Level: Surface World
World Realm: Home
Participation Mode: Embodied Witness
Involvement Level: Passive
Population Level: Populated
Direction of Focus: Right
Consciousness: I-Maginal

Day 1, continued: "The Sitting Watchers"

As my meditation session continued, some sounds soon interrupted my tranquil state. I still felt as if I was in my room meditating, but I sensed the presence of others. I heard two men moving around near my right front side. They seemed to be in the process of dragging chairs closer to me. There actually were two chairs in my room in the area where I heard the sounds. The men were saying they wanted to get the best position for observing the effectiveness of my meditation and were discussing how close to me to move the chairs. Eventually they came to a solution that satisfied them, and they settled down.

While I was hearing all this, I kept absolutely still and continued my routine as if nothing had happened, not wanting to be judged less than adequate in my new Practice. I didn't want them to think I had lost concentration and was eavesdropping on their private conversation. I felt they were close, as if they were sitting right next to me. Without moving my head I opened my eyes, looking at the bookcase and other familiar objects before me. I was reassured by the seeming ordinariness of the scene. This was still my room. All was as it should be. I hoped they hadn't noticed my eyes opening.

But then I realized something was a little off. The shapes and layout weren't quite right. The angles were a little askew. The colors were too saturated. That's when it hit me. I shouldn't be seeing this scene. The lights were out and the room should be dark. I wasn't seeing my real room. Where was I? Ironically, these thoughts were what shattered the illusion. Apparently I wasn't troubled by the presence of two strangers in my room. I even wanted to perform well for them, as though I was being tested. But when I opened what I thought were my eyes and noticed the lights were on, that discovery brought me back to my senses. I was unceremoniously yanked out of this phantom world and deposited back in my old room, where I did my best to continue my Practice in spite of being somewhat perplexed by all that had transpired. A little later the timer went off and my first meditative experience was over. I had much to think about.

Commentary

The experiences from my first day of meditation were surprising in several ways. Based on my earlier attempts so many years before, I had expected the actual act of sitting in meditation to be much more difficult. Instead, I found the physical act to be very natural and comfortable. Time seemed to go by much more quickly than I had anticipated. I never found myself wondering how much longer I would have to sit there. I was surprised when the timer went off signaling the end of the session.

Although I carried no preconceptions about what kinds of inner experiences I would have during my first session, the ones I did have were not ones I could ever have foreseen. The clarity and vividness of the experiences I encountered were unlike anything I had experienced before. Certainly at the time that should have made more of an impact on me than it did. I don't really know why I was so nonchalant about what I had just experienced. I was apparently more concerned about interpreting the meaning of the experience than I was about the raw fact of having had it.

While the appearance of the photo presented a puzzle needing to be solved, the episode of the two observers was even more enigmatic. My assumption at the time was that they were figments of my imagination, as if thinking that somehow explained anything. As if asking myself the question, "Did that really happen or was it just my imagination?" made any sense. After all, who did I think was going to answer that question beyond the voice of the very faculty whose trustworthiness I was questioning? In my mind, the experience I had of the Sitting Watchers was a real experience, one that actually happened. The sounds I heard were real sounds, the voices real voices.

My ultimate source of doubt wasn't whether this experience occurred, but rather about the reality of what the experience purported to show. Were there in fact two people sitting next to me who were the cause of the sounds I was hearing, whom I would have seen had I just slightly turned my head and looked in their direction? Even if I had turned and seen them, would they have been real entities, present as spirits or autonomous agents of the Soul, with their own internal lives and thoughts, or would they instead have been just hollow shells, some fantasy conjured up by my unconscious?

In addition, if I had seen them there, where exactly was there? Where was I when I confidently believed I was sitting in my chair meditating under the watchful gaze of two unseen agents? I certainly believed I was still in my room. There was nothing about the feelings and thoughts I was having at the time that gave me any cause to question that, at least not until later when I opened what I thought were my eyes. But of course I wasn't in the same room where I began meditating that morning and to which I would subsequently return. I was in my room, but it was a different room and maybe also I was a different I. These were certainly different kinds of eyes.

Rationalizing It All Away

My attempt at rationalizing away the impact of this experience at the time went something like this. I knew I had been very skeptical about my ability to successfully undertake any meditative practice. I believed I would only make progress at meditation if I could dispel my doubts. The presence of the two observers in my second vision may have represented my mind's attempt to externalize these doubts by giving them form. That I wanted to perform well for them showed that I wanted to prove to myself that this was something I could do. If I could successfully continue in spite of the presence of the observers, maybe that would enable me to gain needed confidence.

As plausible as this seemed to me at the time, I was not entirely comfortable with all of its details. In particular, the question of why two figures appeared rather than just one puzzled me. I quickly dismissed the idea there was a simple pattern here, as in: first vision, one figure, second vision, two.

Why did it take two people to watch me meditate? In my real-world experience, when I was being evaluated, it was usually by a single authority figure, like a teacher or a judge. It was true that parents represented a case when more than one person was involved. But in my vision, both figures were male. I did not recall being in situations where two men sat in such intimate judgment of me.

It was quite possible I was overthinking this at the time. There was one obvious explanation why two observers were present in my vision. On my right there were exactly two chairs next to where I was sitting. This does ignore the question of why these observers would need to be seated in order to perform their vigil over my meditation.

My First Test

This issue of how much monitoring was required highlighted another odd feature of this situation. The two men seemed to be involved in a discussion about how close to sit to me. They acted as if they needed to be close enough to observe more than just my posture and breathing. It was as if they were trying to somehow monitor my thoughts by peering into my head.

Strangely, at no time in their discussion did they seem concerned their presence would disturb me. Nor did I get the impression that they wanted to sit next to me for the explicit purpose of testing my concentration. They weren't saying, "Let's see how close we can get before he notices us." They just assumed I would not detect their presence. They must have believed themselves to be in another dimension imperceptible by me. Perhaps it was a good thing that I had enough sense not to reveal I was on to them.

Or, perhaps it wasn't. More likely, given my subsequent experiences, they were there to conduct a test to determine if, in fact, I would be able to perceive their presence. If so, my decision to ignore them might have been precisely the wrong reaction on my part. My attempt to pass what I thought was the test might have resulted in my failing the real test. Of course, if they really could see into my thoughts, they would know I had detected their presence. Presumably, if I had passed their test, they would be back.

The Vignette Motif

This vision is a good example of the Vignette motif, which is primarily distinguished by the nature of my role as observer. Unlike the Visage motif, in cases of the Vignette motif I would be present and embodied within the scope of the vision, though only as a stationary and passive observer. I would remain disengaged from the situation, sometimes due to an intentional choice on my part and other times due to the situation in which I found myself. Because I was internal to the vision, the scenario would unfold before me without my involvement.

The other important characteristic of this type of motif is the activity of other individuals who are typically in conversation with each other in the midst of a brief encounter. Although I would not be actively engaged with the unfolding scenario, my presence would still be an integral part of the content of the vision. The other actors in the vision might be aware of me and by their actions acknowledge my presence, even if no direct interaction took place between us. Or they might act as if they had no sense of my presence at all. In either case I would still feel a sense of connection with what was transpiring before me and less like someone surreptitiously spying on a private conversation.

The Home Realm and Human Domain

Because this vision took place in the Home realm, many of its features were very familiar to those found in my everyday life. The Home realm represents the visionary expression of the world closest and most accessible to normal everyday experiences. It's the world "right next door." This was the answer to my earlier question about where I was when I saw the Watchers in the vision. But this wasn't an answer I had available to me at the time.

As my experiences from my first day of meditation revealed, the Home realm was the first place my visions brought me when I first began the Practice. Sometimes, as in this case, I was seemingly still in my meditation room. When I found myself in this realm, I felt like I was still in the normal world, at least until I began to notice the subtle and then later the not so subtle discrepancies. Shapes were a little too fuzzy, straight edges a little too rounded, colors a little too saturated, lighting a little off. And yet it still felt very familiar and comfortable to me.

Similarly, the Human domain includes the elements we typically encounter in our normal comings and goings. Visions in this domain occurred within or around structures explicitly constructed by people. These kinds of components would all indicate the influence of the human element. It is not surprising that many of my visions were to take place within this domain.

9. Techniques for Quieting the Mind

Refining the Practice

On my second day of Practice I decided to increase the length of the meditation period to forty minutes, since the thirty minutes had gone by quickly for me. Other than that I intended to follow the same regimen as I had the day before. I would begin at approximately the same time in the morning. The sequence of background music playing on the Internet radio station would be different though, since its playlist didn't seem to have any recognizable pattern.

While sitting in meditation the second day, I immediately noticed my mind was more active than it had been the day before. I still focused on the shapes and patterns moving behind my closed eyelids. But the thoughts drifting through my awareness seemed more defined than they had been the previous day. Then they had seemed faint and distant. Today these thoughts demanded my attention. I would need another approach to successfully quiet my mind.

Before starting the Practice I had reviewed different techniques for quieting the mind. Among the most common ones described for closed eye meditation are following your breaths in and out, repeatedly counting the number of your breaths from 1 to 10, intoning a mantric sound like "OM," etc. These kinds of approaches are intended to lure the mind into quietude by distracting it with a never-ending string of repetitive tasks.

More philosophical approaches include focusing on paradoxical Zen-type riddles, such as "Where were you before you were born?" or "What is the sound of one hand clapping?" Other examples are "Who is it that is having these experiences?" or "If all things return to the One, where does the One return to?" Much of the effectiveness of these techniques stems from their ability to preoccupy the mind with seemingly unanswerable and possibly nonsensical questions. Of course, the hidden intent of this method is that the meditator will, after a long period of contemplating the riddle, obtain sudden insight.

Another common piece of advice for the beginning meditator is to simply observe thoughts as they come and go without attaching any significance to them. Otherwise, the meta-act of thinking about thoughts will initiate an ever-expanding cascade of additional thoughts about thoughts. The implicit assumption is that the mind stores thoughts in a background repository while waiting to express them. Once this accumulated backlog is released, the production of new thoughts will slow down dramatically. This will be particularly true without the multiplier effect of attention being paid to them. The success of this approach depends on maintaining a separation between the author and the perceiver of these thoughts.

Quieting the Senses

All the above approaches are offered as techniques for quieting the mind. But their importance in the success of the new meditator does not end there. When successfully applied they don't just dampen the stream of thoughts and images coming from the mind. They also help suppress the equally noisy input from the external senses, including the sensations from the body sitting in meditation.

For example, two of the techniques I use in my Practice are explicitly directed at minimizing the contribution of the major senses of vision and hearing to consciousness. They do this by focusing those senses on unstructured inputs.

In the visual case, by focusing my attention on the chaotic milieu of dark shifting shapes behind my closed eyelids, no coherent information is presented to consciousness. There are no persisting patterns to follow or anticipate. The experience is very similar to what I imagine being immersed inside a lava lamp would have been like.

The ambient music I play in the background has similar characteristics. By intention, ambient music offers amorphous, atmospheric elements in place of the traditional musical features of structure and rhythm. There are no recognizable melodies to capture your attention or create expectations about what you would hear next.

Both of these techniques work because human sensory processing systems have evolved to identify shapes and patterns. By depriving these systems of ordered data, the contribution of their input to awareness is decreased. Unstructured experiences are pushed into the background of consciousness. Based on my previous attempts at listening to music from other cultures, what experiences count as structured or unstructured certainly have a strong cultural component to them.

Inside the Bubble

While sitting in meditation that second day, I did discover a new faculty I could use in my Practice. The experiences from the first day had apparently left my mind still actively pondering possible meanings and interpretations. This meditative state in which sensory input is suppressed is a very tempting place for reflecting on experiences without the interruption of everyday distractions. That was the situation in which I found myself as I tried to relax into meditative consciousness.

Since attempting to mentally relax did not seem to be working, I decided to try active engagement instead. I focused on attempting to keep my mind clear of thoughts. I did not employ the often-parodied strategy of telling myself not to think of anything. I did not try to shut down my thoughts. My focus was instead on controlling how much of this output actually made it into my awareness. My assumption was that these thoughts were not my own. Because they came from somewhere else, I should be able to resist their entry.

After some experimentation I came up with a visualization technique that prevented thoughts from entering my consciousness. The manner in which I did this may not work for everyone, but it did seem effective for me. I imagined I could materialize a small balloon within the center of the dark three-dimensional sphere of my consciousness. The walls of the balloon behaved as a membrane that allowed the diminished ambient contributions of my senses to pass into awareness but not structured material such as thoughts or ideas. As I slowly inflated the balloon and widened the range of its influence, the various streams of thoughts were pushed further and further back towards the outer periphery of my consciousness until they ultimately became too faint to discern.

The Gatekeeper, A New Muscle

I felt I had just discovered a new capability I did not know I had, what I call the "gatekeeper," since its purpose was to control the kinds of content allowed to enter consciousness. We all have the ability to focus our attention on certain features in the external world or widen our attention to take in more of the landscape. It is something we do quite naturally. This process was similar to that, except in this case the widening of attention took place in the inner world and required an act of concentration to achieve. It felt similar to a physical gesture, as if I were inflating my lungs, or more apropos, holding open the lids to some inner eye.

I hoped this new internal capacity would become as natural for me as its counterpart was in the external world. As long as I was able to concentrate on the expansion of the imaginary balloon, I could quiet the stream of thoughts. With continued practice I hoped this would become an instinctive part of my meditation, as when an action through repetition becomes a habit and eventually a reflex.

Employing this technique allowed me to once again sink down into a deeper state of meditation. Even though it initially required an internal focus to achieve, the effort did not impact my ability to relax my body. My breathing slowed and became shallower. The sound of the music faded further into the background and the dark shapes swirling in my visual field seemed to acquire an element of transparency . . .

10. Vision 3: *The Standing Watchers*

Vision Matrix

Thematic Narrative: Initiation 3 of 5
Session Cluster: 1 of 1
Motif Elements: Vignette, Dialogue, & Vigil

Subject: Identity, Thinking, Myself, Embodied
Content: Visual, Background, Depth, Animated
Domain: Human

World Level: Surface World
World Realm: Home
Participation Mode: Embodied Witness
Involvement Level: Passive
Population Level: Populated
Direction of Focus: Left
Consciousness: I-Maginal

Day 2: "The Standing Watchers"

After a little while had passed I once again heard two voices engaged in conversation, as I had the day before. This time the voices appeared to be coming from my left front area. The topic of the conversation was different as well. They were discussing what advice they could give me to help me with my meditation. These remarks weren't being addressed to me, nor did they seem to reflect any awareness that I might be listening to them. As before, it was as if they were in a place where they could observe me but assumed I wouldn't see or hear them.

At this point I would like to say I opened my eyes. But that would assume I had a sense of being in willed control of my body, which I did not. I did feel like I was sitting in my meditation chair, so at least to that extent, I felt some degree of solidity and embodiment. But I also felt somewhat separated from my body, as I might if my body had become numb. Rather than turning my body and opening my eyes, I somehow directed my awareness in their direction. I'd say this felt like an example of remote seeing, except for the fact they were right next to me.

What I saw were two men on my left, both in their thirties or early forties, standing and slowly pacing around in front of me. Sometimes they had their arms folded across their chests. Occasionally one of them would bring a hand up to his face and peer in towards me, as if lost in thought while studying me. Other times they would gesture in my direction with their palms upraised as they spoke. They were in a room that was a rough facsimile of the one in which I had begun meditating. While I did not notice it at the time, the dimensions of the room were definitely askew, even though the room's furnishings were in their correct places. There was more space in the room to my left than there should have been, probably in order to provide a sufficient area for the activities of these two men.

I tried to get a good look at their features so I would recognize them if I saw them again. The one on the right looked a little like a considerably younger version of me, with brown hair and a slim build, dressed comfortably, with a checkered plaid shirt with an open collar and jeans. The other had darker features and was probably of African-American descent. He was a little stockier than the first man and had short black hair. He wore a long-sleeved white jersey. I remember being surprised they were dressed so informally. I thought, "So that's what you wear to a vision?"

Fig. 12. The Standing Watchers

The kinds of thoughts I was having indicated I remembered my prior day's encounter with the Watchers, whom I assumed were these same two individuals. I was apparently trying to apply what I had learned from their first visit. But that didn't mean I was thinking this world or these men were somehow less real, or even that this wasn't the same room in which I sat down to meditate that morning. Like the previous day's vision, I was still completely committed to the reality and even the normalcy of the situation in which I found myself. I knew I was meditating and believed what I was experiencing was just the sort of thing one would expect to happen.

My belief that I was still sitting in meditation was the driving force behind my heightened interest in the possible future identities of these two men. I got the impression they might play a role in my later spiritual evolution. Perhaps I would encounter them at a meditative study group or ashram or temple. If I did, having remembered them from this vision, that would be a sign of a situation I should pursue further. While having these thoughts, the timer went off and the two men vanished. I found myself once more back in my room, my second day of meditation over. Once again I was left with more questions than answers.

Commentary

Later that day I pondered the meaning of the two observers. The vision from the previous day had seemingly returned, as if it resumed from the point where it had been interrupted. I took the reappearance of the two Watchers to mean I had passed whatever test they had subjected me to.

There were several differences between the two encounters. Yesterday, the two had been on my right, were sitting, and were discussing how best to observe me. Today they were on my left, were standing, and were discussing how best to help me. The implication seemed to be that having observed and evaluated me the first day, they had identified areas of my practice that needed improvement and were considering how to begin the process of further training. But training for what? I wondered where the meeting had taken place where they discussed my first day's Practice.

The fact they were now standing seemed important. It might have indicated a transition to a more active engagement on their part, given that they wanted to help me. Or it may have been simply due to the fact there were no chairs on that side of the room. My mind might have been attempting to integrate the experience of the observers as seamlessly as possible with my normal everyday life.

The question of why the two were now on my left side is more interesting. One possible interpretation might reflect a certain psychological theory about the lateralization of brain function. In this theory, the two hemispheres of the brain have different kinds of capabilities (McGilchrist 2010). The left hemisphere, which controls the right side of the body, is usually the more dominant side in terms of handedness. It is associated with the logical and analytical functions of the brain. This was consistent with yesterday's vision in which the two were involved in a more clinical observational posture. The right hemisphere, on the other hand, which controls the left side of the body, is associated with the more creative, emotional and holistic capacities of the brain. These capabilities were more representative of the type of supportive and enabling role the two were considering today.

Yin and Yang

Another possible interpretation for the right versus left orientation involves the Chinese philosophy of Yin-Yang. Yin and Yang represent forces in the natural world that appear to be polar opposites of each other, but actually they are the complementary forces constituting a unified, evolving, and dynamic system. Neither force is ever entirely pure. Each always contains some amount of its opposite.

Many common dualities in the world are viewed as manifestations of the polarity between Yin and Yang, including female and male, dark and light, yielding and firm, down and up, left and right, hidden and overt, etc. As one polarity went to the extreme, it would turn into its opposite. The Chinese characters for Yin and Yang represent respectively the shady and the sunny sides of a hill. It is one and the same hill. Only the illumination has changed. Yin and Yang are key concepts within Taoism, as expressed in this line from chapter 1:

> *"Hidden and manifest received different names,*
> *But as one sprung forth from creation."*

Fig. 13. The T'ai Chi (Yin-Yang) Diagram

Since I had been actively involved in the study of Taoism and Chinese martial arts, it is possible that something of this philosophy entered into the duality of these two visions. On one day the figures were visible and on the other day not. On one day the figures were seated and on the other day standing. On one day they were on the right side and on the other day on the left side. On one day I felt I had a body and on the other day I did not. On one day I had a passive attitude and on the other a more active one. And finally, there were two figures involved, one with lighter skin and the other with darker. Perhaps the two visions were presented to me in this manner to symbolically represent the other fundamental duality manifested in my practice of meditation: the contrast between the outer world of the senses and the inner world of the Soul.

The other differences that occurred involved my own deportment within the visions. On the previous day I felt as if I were actually sitting in the room and being evaluated. This was why I did not move my head to look at the observers. I still felt the presence of my body, and when I looked towards the bookcase in front of me, I felt as if I had opened my eyes. Today, on the other hand, I felt a diminished bodily presence and directed my gaze in their direction by a simple act of will.

My thoughts were also different. Rather than interpreting the visitation as a test, I was now comfortable enough with their presence to actively attempt to remember details about their appearance. I was willing to consider the possibility that I needed to see them in order to acquire information that might help me in the future. Their appearance had taken on for me the same status as the enigmatic photo from the previous day's experience. Both were potential clues to solving unknown mysteries.

The Vignette Motif (again)

The motif and its accompanying properties for this vision are, unsurprisingly, very similar to those for the "Sitting Watchers" vision. Even though I directed my gaze in this vision to look at and think about the identities and behaviors of the visitors, my behavior was essentially passive, indicative of the Vignette motif. This was because I still continued to sit perfectly still and made no attempt to move any part of my body. I was frozen. I did not try to attract their attention or engage them in conversation. They continued to behave as if I had no cognizance of their presence.

In retrospect, maybe one of the reasons they did not show any acknowledgement of my awareness of them was precisely because of my demonstrated passivity. Maybe that is another one of the laws of this visionary realm that guides the behaviors of observers. Unless the subject makes an attempt to explicitly engage you, ignore any signs of the subject's awareness of your presence. This is, in fact, one of the teachings of the shamanic tradition.

The Possibility of Foresight

My willingness to think, months before the Aurobindo revelation, that I was potentially receiving clues about events that had not yet occurred revealed something about my philosophical worldview. First, it indicated that I believed, even as I was starting meditation, in the possibility of foreknowledge about the future. You couldn't receive clues about what to look for in the future unless time was a lot more curved than it appeared. Second, it acknowledged the existence of unknown forces able and willing to disseminate this knowledge, whether they were ones hidden in my own unconscious or somewhere external to me. Whichever was the case, it did not occur to me to question their underlying motivations or identities.

A few events in my past may help explain why I would consider the possibility of foresight even before beginning my meditative practice. Most people have probably had a few psychic experiences in which they believed they had a premonition of an event before it happened. I was no exception. While my experiences in this realm were remarkably mundane compared to most, they were still unusual enough to remember.

The first happened one summer when I was a teenager. A local radio station was having a contest. Once a day a caller tried to guess a number between one and a hundred based on a random drawing. Every time an incorrect guess was made, more money was added to the pot. Needless to say, the prize amount grew quite large as the summer wore on.

Towards the end of the summer I was driving home one day from the local lake (Lake Massapoag, said to have once been the site of one of Paul Revere's mines) half-listening to the radio. The announcer came on and said they would be taking another caller for the contest. Suddenly the number "67" popped into my head. I thought nothing of it at the time. Then the caller came on the radio and guessed "67." I thought "What a coincidence." Then the announcer screamed, "You've won! You've won!"

I was surprised and more than a little chagrined, just as I imagined the station manager was who had assumed no one would ever guess the right number that summer. This event predisposed me to view claims of psychic phenomena with a little less skepticism.

The Mundane and the Terrifying

The next time something similar to this happened was in my late thirties. It also involved a broadcast (is there a pattern here?), but it was from television rather than radio. I don't remember exactly what I was doing, but a lawyer show was playing in the background on the television. As I recall the plot, a teacher had been accused of murdering one of his young students. It was the defense attorney's turn to present his opening statement. Suddenly, for no particular reason, I blurted out the words, "A terrible crime has been committed." Several seconds later, the exact same words came from the television, with the same intonation and delivery. Since I was alone at the time, I had no one with whom to share my incredulity.

This same phenomenon has occurred many dozens of times since then, usually in the presence of witnesses who were impressed by my parlor tricks. The problem was I had no control of my prescience. It only occurred when my attention was directed at something other than the television show. But on those occasions when it happened, it was an exact match in all respects to what was said in the broadcast.

When I consciously attempted, as people sometimes do while watching a familiar show, to mouth the words simultaneously with the actor, I would never get them quite right. I was only successful when my attention was distracted, possibly because my consciousness was open to incursion by some prescient force from the realms of the unconscious.

Taoists would describe these events as good illustrations of the concept of "*wu wei*," or what they called "non-action." They would say I only succeeded in these cases because I didn't try, because I acted without desire or attention. As Lao Tzu says in chapter 37 of the *Tao-Te-Ching*,

> "*The Tao is always without-acting (wu wei),*
> *But it is not inactive.*
> *If princes and kings were similarly able to guard it,*
> *The 10,000 things would change on their own.*
> *If men become changed by the desire to do,*
> *I would calm them with no-names' simplicity.*
> *By calming them with no-names' simplicity,*
> *Men would not desire.*
> *Not with desire, but with silence,*
> *Will Heaven and Earth correct themselves.*"

If these events represented a psychic ability, that ability is the most mundane one imaginable, unless, of course, I wanted to go to Hollywood and become a screenwriter. But they did further strengthen my belief that certain kinds of psychic phenomena were real. A few of these kinds of events might be explained by a combination of coincidence and an innate ability for screenwriting. But mere coincidence or skill would not explain the long string of these that occurred off and on over several decades.

Since I have started meditating, this phenomenon no longer occurs. But new ones have begun to surface within meditational states of consciousness. Most significantly, about seven months into my practice I experienced something very disturbing while meditating, when I heard a very loud explosion that shook me violently out of my trance in Threshold consciousness. The explosion was very similar in power to the one from the "Cosmic

Echoes" dream and, as it turned out, foretold a similar kind of fiery cataclysm. I found the experience deeply troubling, since it reminded me of the 2009 science fiction movie *Knowing*. I remember saying to my wife that day that I hoped this didn't mean an airplane was going to crash. The next day I learned of the explosion of Malaysia Airlines Flight 17. That event not only cemented my belief in the possibility of people being able to obtain glimpses of events from the future, but also in the power of meditation to awaken those powers.

Radio Head

There is another possible line of explanation for these pre-meditational experiences that doesn't require the existence of foreknowledge, though I'm not sure it's any more plausible within a conventional worldview. The radio and television examples both involved the transmission of electromagnetic waves. Rather than having foreknowledge of what I was going to hear from the devices that received the transmissions, this new approach holds that my senses can function as their own receiver and tuner, bypassing the electronic gadgetry.

This assumes the existence of currently unknown sensory capacities. Think of them functioning as part of a highly sophisticated signal processing system, capturing, translating and relaying the broadcasts directly to the area of the brain that controls speech output. Since the brain would know what was going to be said, it could simultaneously relay that as spoken sound directly into awareness. If the timing were just right, I would hear my own spoken words before those of the radio or television broadcast.

The Psychic Security Agency

While this approach is intriguing and might explain away the psychic experiences in my past, it doesn't provide any insight into the meaning of the two Watchers or my feeling that their presence was intended to provide me with clues about the future. There are certainly alternative interpretations from other traditions that might be relevant here.

A psychologist might say they are a manifestation of unconscious desires to succeed in meditation. These forces were attempting to boost my confidence and give me new reasons to continue. A Jungian might describe the visitors as archetypal forms from the collective unconscious appearing in the guise of wise sages to give me access to the accumulated wisdom of the ages. Neither of these psychological interpretations felt right, especially since my visitors didn't seem particularly wise. If truth be told, they appeared more Rosencrantz-and-Guildensternesque than they did Svengali-like. These were no masters of the universe.

A more radical interpretation asserts that these were not the manifestations of unconscious drives but in fact actual visitors from other non-human realms. Many religions and esoteric traditions describe the existence of hierarchies of beings, who have the mission of observing and helping us. These kinds of belief are apparently widespread in contemporary American culture. Opinion polls have revealed, for example, that a majority of the American public believes in the existence of guardian angels that appear at critical moments in our lives, often in human form, to guide us or save us from harm. Were these two my guardian angels?

Shamanistic teachings, such as those associated with Michael Harner, would maintain these two beings were helping spirits inhabiting the Middle World. These beings appeared to help seekers in their journeying and spiritual evolution. Ancient forms of Chinese or Buddhist philosophy also referred to these kinds of beings as spirits though, of course, their appearance, dress and behaviors would be quite different than how they appeared to me, given the cultural differences. The ancient Greeks called them "*daemons.*"

My experiences with the Watchers, however, didn't really seem to fit these traditions, especially given their seeming ignorance of my awareness of them. Or perhaps it was merely indifference? The fact that these beings made no effort to communicate with me or acknowledge my presence certainly raises questions about what kinds of assistance they were intending to provide. But perhaps I didn't know the whole story.

Other modern occult traditions speak of the existence of secret societies of illuminated individuals who have the ability to observe and project themselves into the minds of others. If these societies exist, perhaps they are able to monitor on a regular basis the activity of individuals engaged in meditation in order to identify those who they feel should be watched or even recruited, in their role as the security agency for psychic communications. Maybe this group would be called the "PSA" (Psychic Security Agency).

I only hope if such societies exist, they would quickly find me uninteresting and concentrate on more deserving candidates. I certainly do not consider myself secret society material. Indeed, the fact that I am so willing to discuss these events shows my inherent unsuitability for membership. Remember, the first and second rules of Fight Club (from the movie of the same name) are "You do not talk about Fight Club." Coincidentally, many spiritual teachers impose a similar rule on their students, with one exception: "You do not talk about your meditation, except to me."

If other spiritual worlds and beings really do exist, I believe the much-needed spiritual evolution of the human race would be better served by the widespread dissemination of this knowledge rather than the systematic suppression so dogmatically pursued throughout history. By the way, if there are any spiritual beings listening, that message is for you.

Mystery Solved? A Grimm Discovery

As in the case of the "Ghost Guru" vision, it was some time before the identity of the individuals in my vision was revealed to me. Clairvoyance, it turned out, had nothing to do with it. Surprisingly, these individuals, unlike the case of the young Aurobindo, turned out to be fictional. It was almost a year and a half before I recognized who they were.

This occurred at a time when I was looking for these individuals in my normal life as I attended various kinds of spiritual gatherings. My discovery of the Aurobindo connection with my first vision had instilled in me a constant sense of vigilance and strengthened my determination to locate the two Watchers should they pass through my life. Needless to say, I was somewhat disappointed when I discovered their fictional identity, not in some great work of fiction, but instead as the lead characters of a mildly entertaining NBC TV fantasy series, *Grimm*.

The show portrays the adventures of a mythical supernatural enforcer, Nick Burkhardt, working as a homicide detective in Portland, Oregon (the Santa Cruz of the Northwest) with his partner Hank Griffin. As the show's title suggests, Nick discovered he was a descendent of the fabled Grimm family popularized through the collection of fairy tales bearing their name. In the TV series, these stories weren't just fairy tales. They were the real accounts of the activities of hidden beings lurking among us, which on the show were called "*wesen*" (from the German word for "creature").

These creatures, once worshipped as God-like beings in ancient times, appear in our time as ordinary humans until they transform through a process known as "*woging*" into their hidden animal-like form. Nick, the Grimm descendant, is the only one able to see them in their true form prior to their completed transformation. Not all *wesen* are evil on the show. Many had allied themselves with Nick against the more dangerous forms of these creatures, wanting to live, like so many of us, a normal and peaceful life with their true natures safely hidden.

Since I had seen episodes of this show prior to encountering these two characters in my vision as the Watchers, I was surprised it took me so long to recognize the correlation. It was as if I had been under some mental block that hid their identity from me, like some psychic Chinese wall erected between two regions of my consciousness in order to keep them apart.

Had I recognizing the Grimm actors at the time, I would have been spared the effort of that yearlong search to locate them in the comings and goings of my daily life. But maybe that was the point. Maybe my spiritual evolution required a heightened degree of daily vigilance in the so-called normal world. The incident of the "Shaggy Dog" certainly acted to make that point, as did several other events that followed the episode I called "The Awakening."

There is another possible reason why I had been blocked from this recognition until after some critical number of visions had occurred. By this point the number of visions appearing within the Practice had significantly declined. Perhaps I wouldn't recognize the meaning hidden within my vision's Grimm presentation until after I accumulated a sufficient catalog of visionary experiences. If this was so, then what was the message I was meant to find?

One of the key themes of the Grimm television show is that hidden among us is a type of parahuman, a human-animal hybrid, who is able to move both its consciousness and bodily form from one mode of being to another. Was this a type of metaphorical foreshadowing, albeit one I would only recognize after the fact, about the theme expressed by many of my visions? Was I, in my visions, destined to play the role of the mythological *wesen*?

If the answers to any of these questions are "yes," then my visions will have a particular type of tale to tell me. They will show my bodily form and consciousness morphing into those of other beings. They will reveal a visionary power of shape shifting and consciousness jumping, perhaps one the Watchers recognized and wanted to nurture. If these kinds of events occur, I will have to confront their implications for my evolving views about consciousness and the Self.

11. More Philosophy: The Paradox of the Tao

Lessons from the Tao

Let It Be

Fresh from the surreal experiences of the previous two days, I had perhaps formed unrealistic expectations about what subsequent meditation sessions would bring. I imagined I might be visited again by the two mysterious figures or receive further clues about the enigmatic photo. Perhaps I would see strange new apparitions. I started looking forward to each session in the same way as I might the airing of a new episode of a favorite TV show.

But meditative visions do not have a constant cast of characters or recognizable locales like a TV series. There were no program directors, no plots, and no actors in my Practice, at least none discernible at this early stage. Only time would tell if there was an unfolding narrative at work. Nor were different states of consciousness like television channels. There was no schedule for what program would be playing on what channel when.

If there was one lesson I learned early on in my Practice, it was that the appearance of meditative experiences would follow no easily discernable rules. Similar to an old water heater, some times meditation would run hot, other times cold. Probably the worst thing I could do for the viability of my practice was to become attached to the experiences I was having. I needed to let them go and not treat them as private, precious possessions. I'm hoping that publicly writing about these experiences and trying to understand their intent is one good way of doing this. Many in the mindfulness movement would probably disagree with this prescription, however.

It is easy to forget that meditation is very sensitive to the state of mind of the practitioner. It behaves sometimes like a kind of psychic vortex, one that swallows up all the expectations and feelings it encounters. My hopes and desires for certain results were the wrong kinds of ingredients to be feeding it. Any attempt to intentionally shape the meditative experiences will contaminate the integrity of the process with unnecessary psychic "flak."

This is the major reason I do not believe in the viability of the guided meditations that are in such widespread use in mindfulness training. The experiences that resulted would not be generated spontaneously by your unconscious but instead would follow the scenarios described in the guided session. The speaker's voice would control your narrative, not your Soul. Your unconscious would be the *instrument*, rather than the *musician*.

I am willing to concede that forms of shamanic practice in which seekers pose questions to their "spirits" before entering trance states can communicate with elements of the unconscious. However, based on my experiences, I don't believe these kinds of methods will access the deeper states. Jung certainly believed in the viability of some kinds of self-guided visions. In *The Red Book* he described some of his experiences as resulting from *incubation dreams*, which embodied the thoughts he was having before he fell asleep. In general, though, I believe it is best to let the Soul have its say.

Vessels of the Spirit

Chapter 29 of the *Tao-Te-Ching* provides warnings to the seeker about these kinds of attempts to influence the outcomes of meditation, whether they involve forming expectations or trying to direct results. These are warnings every practitioner must continually struggle to heed. I am as guilty as any of trying to hold onto my experiences while they were happening, or of forming expectations about what kinds of experiences I would like to have. I still struggle with these things and probably always will. Chapter 29 also depicts the ways sequences of visionary experiences can appear to the seeker. This is my rendering.

> *"Seek to hold celestial things*
> *You will never find success.*
> *Celestial things can only be held*
> *By the Vessels the Spirits express.*
> *With act you can try to make them,*
> *The Vessels will always shatter.*
> *By grip you can try to hold them,*
> *The Spirits will all just scatter.*

These things appear in many ways:
Some will lead; others follow.
Some will raise themselves up high,
Others left unsown stay fallow.
Some will softly whisper and hiss,
Others will shout and bellow.
Some penetrate through with strength,
Others too weak just wallow.
A person sacred sage can become
If he seeks no measure of excess,
Gives up all extravagant pursuit,
Dreams no more of grand success."

This passage is a beautiful expression of the Taoist doctrine that meditative experiences need to be allowed to happen *spontaneously*, without expectation or direction.

Quieting Body Talk

For reasons unknown to me, the next few days of the Practice brought no new vivid visions or visitations by strange beings. Part of me was certainly disappointed. Were the first two days similar to an exciting movie trailer that lured you into the theater only to discover too late that the previews were the best part of the movie? I realized that although meditation might sometimes be enjoyable, it couldn't be sought as entertainment without becoming a shallow caricature of itself. The fact that I had that attitude, no matter how short-lived it might have been, shows why it is so difficult for media-saturated Americans, among whom I must count myself, to successfully persist in a long-term, gradually unfolding practice such as meditation.

Even in the absence of new iconic visual experiences towards the end of this first week, I was able to learn more about the process of what it took to successfully relax into meditation. I have already spoken about the process of quieting the mind and dampening the contributions from the external senses. Another key element for entering into the meditative state was the importance of quieting the sensations received from the body.

When I first sat down in my chair to begin meditation and closed my eyes, the strongest set of sensations I received was from my physical body. A whole constellation of feelings besieged me:

83

my forearms resting on my legs, my hands touching, my feet on the floor, the Zen pillow resting against my back, the chair beneath me, etc. I felt the front of my body rising and falling with each breath and the air moving in and out of my nose. I struggled to keep my head balanced in an upright position.

There were several things I had to do in order to successfully quiet these sensations, though "do" is probably the wrong word. A better way of putting it would be to say I allowed a sequence of progressive relaxations to occur that caused these feelings to diminish and slowly disappear.

First, by keeping my body absolutely still and letting gravity pull it into the chair, all my muscle tension began to disappear. To the extent this was an action, it was strictly an action of letting go. My many years of *t'ai chi ch'uan* practice were useful here, since they had trained me in the art of finding and releasing areas of tension in my body. Hatha yoga would also be effective in this regard.

The Taoist paradox here was that only by letting myself become heavy would my body become light. As the first line of chapter 26 of the *Tao-Te-Ching* says, "*The heavy becomes the root of the light, the tranquil becomes the ruler of the agitated.*" Lao Tzu also spoke of the importance of letting the flow of energies go downward, as in the first line of chapter 66, "*Rivers and seas can be kings of the hundred valleys because they are good at flowing downwards.*" A similar sentiment is expressed in the last line of chapter 32: "*Tao in the world is like valley streams flowing into rivers and seas.*" So it was with my tension. I had to let it drain from my body like a downward flowing liquid.

The other important part of this process involved my breath. Instead of using directed breathing exercises such as the ones in *pranayama* or *ch'i kung* that many people employed in their meditation, my experience led me to a different approach. For me the opposite of controlled, conscious breathing was critical. My breathing needed to remain completely uncontrolled, but also as soft and quiet as possible. Controlled breathing required consciously engaging certain muscle groups, a process contrary to allowing all the muscles to relax. This is precisely the problem with the way meditative breathing is frequently taught in self-help books.

Similarly, in order not to disrupt the condition of stillness I was trying to enter, breathing needed to become so slow and gentle that it disappeared from the attention of the body and physical senses. If you exhaled over the mirror-like surface of a bowl of still water, it would not disturb the surface. This is expressed in chapter 10 of the *Tao-Te-Ching*, which contains passages about breathing so softly that you become like a newborn baby (2nd stanza) and keeping the surface of a mirror free from blemishes (3rd stanza).

Opening Heaven's Gate

Chapter 10 of the *Tao-Te-Ching* provides an extended account of the guidelines for Taoist yoga and the kinds of attitude and approaches you must take for your meditative practice to succeed. The following is my interpretive translation:

"Can Animal (p'o) and Spiritual (ying) Souls
Be embraced as one in your heart?
Can you hold fast to true unity?
Never let it depart?

Can you concentrate Vital Energy (ch'i)?
Exhale your breath so gently,
Become just as soft
As a newborn baby?

Can you wash away all blemishes?
Diminish dualities' bad effects?
Wipe clean the Dark Mirror (hsuan lan),
Remove its lingering defects?

Can you love your people equally?
Make diverse parts a whole?
Find harmony among your members,
Take no action; pursue no goal?

Can you carefully open and close
Heaven's Gate just so wide,
Patiently wait to nest
Like a female bird inside?

Can you successfully travel deeply?
Into the empty whiteness so bright?
Seek no knowledge there,
Nor occult gift from its light?

Then you will birth many wonders
In the secret fields of the Dark.
Create new forms there
Without diminishing their spark.

You will help them all to grow
But never on them depend.
You will develop them fully
But not direct their end.

The names for all these ways
You should always eschew.
Just call them simply,
The Dark Virtue."

Though poetic in nature, this passage lists the many challenges confronting the practitioner attempting to enter into the secret realms of the Tao. It also describes some characteristics of the visions I will be describing, especially with respect to the "empty whiteness," the "fields of the Dark," and the "Dark Mirror."

The Challenge of Staying Awake

To Sleep, Perchance to Dream

I discovered over these next few days that within minutes of successfully stilling my body and quieting my breathing I would sink into short trance-like states. I had no recollection of the transition into these states or any sense of time passing while within them. I did find upon returning that my head typically had tilted slightly forward even though the rest of my body had remained absolutely still. This might be because my head does not normally stay upright without a degree of effort on my part (my *sifu* can attest to this). When I was completely relaxed with no focus on my body, the head would naturally settle into a more stable position.

Clearly, I had some work to do on posture, both in and outside of meditation, especially when it came to that stubborn block of a head. While my head was held perhaps a little too loose, the rest of my body would quickly become frozen and immobile in meditation. After a short period of sitting, the rest of my body would feel numb and vacant, as if it were an inanimate chunk of wood (like *p'u*, the famous uncarved log often spoken of in the *Tao-Te-Ching* as a symbol for the unformed potentiality of the Tao). At this point my awareness would tend to disappear for short periods of time before returning back to this state of deep relaxation, where I would once again find myself present within meditation.

I did not believe I had actually fallen asleep in these trance-like states, even though this was a very common complaint of people new to meditation. If I had, my posture would have deteriorated much more than I experienced. But I do believe this was indicative of my passing through the transitional borderland between wakefulness and deeper states of meditative consciousness. The comparable sleep stage was called by sleep scientists Stage 1 non-REM sleep and was often referred to as "relaxed wakefulness." The type of droopy head I experienced was a very common occurrence in this stage (and in classrooms throughout the world). In the context of meditative awareness I will refer to this particular stage as Threshold consciousness.

During the transition to this comparable stage in sleep, many people experience what is known as a "hypnic jerk," which appears as an involuntary twitch. This is reportedly the body's reaction to discovering it is falling asleep. If I had in fact actually fallen asleep, it was definitely a different mode of sleep than I normally experienced at night lying in bed.

While meditating I repeatedly experienced my own version of these hypnic jerks. Sometimes when I was meditating my jaws and teeth would suddenly click together. What surprised me was that these events occurred during periods when I was definitely still aware of myself as present in meditation. Often these clicks would occur when I was engaged in self-reflection about what I was experiencing or thinking about the meaning of some philosophical passage.

What was different about my experience of these clicks was that they did not initiate any startle reflex or adrenalin surge on my part, as they normally would when occurring outside of meditation.

I would hear and feel these clicks, which would often sound quite loud within my head, but without any impact on the quality of my relaxation or meditative engagement.

Thinking about the phenomenon of these jaw clicks later on, I came to a couple of conclusions, one serious, one not so serious. In the latter case I thought I should create a grading system for evaluating the quality of my meditation based upon how many jaw clicks I had. "Yes, that was just a two click session." "Wow, yesterday I had a four click day!" "No clicks today." More significantly, the existence of these clicks and my anomalous reaction to them provided important confirmation to me that even though my physical body may have entered a transitional zone between wakefulness and sleep, I was still awake and aware of being in a state of meditation.

I conducted a simple experiment to see if I could find another way to test my belief that I wasn't falling asleep. Rather than attempting to stay awake, I tried to see if I could allow myself to fall asleep while meditating. Despite many attempts, I could not. Perhaps falling asleep was another one of those things you could only do when you were not trying, so that the mere intention of wanting to sleep was sufficient to prevent it. That certainly wasn't the case at night in bed, but maybe there was something special about meditation. If so, then I had inadvertently discovered a new technique for not falling asleep during meditation, at least in my own case.

Meeting the Master

I was reminded of an incident that had occurred about ten years or so ago. I was attending a seminar in San Francisco on *t'ai chi ch'uan* being offered by the famous grandmaster Chen Xiao Wang (CXW), who was visiting from the birthplace of the discipline in China, Chen Family Village. CXW instructed us that before we began the practice of the moving form, we should stand immobile in a meditative stance known as "*wu chi*," where we would slow our breathing down as much as possible. He told us to close our eyes and with his arms gently pushing down the air in front of him said, "Calm... down..."

Needless to say, after a few minutes I relaxed to such an extent that my attention was gone from my body, resulting in my body swaying slightly to the back. At that point, much like the Zen master who caught one of his students napping, he gave me a smack on my back. "No sleeping," he said. I knew I hadn't been sleeping, but I'd seen enough kung fu movies to know not to contradict a kung fu master. Still, I thought, even if I were asleep, sleeping while in a standing position would have demonstrated a commendable level of relaxation. Surely I should have been praised. I kept that thought to myself. The next night at the dinner thrown in his honor, every time CXW saw me he would point at me and say, "No sleeping."

Wu Chi: Not Empty but Before

Before I return to my account of the Practice, I should say a little more about the relationship between *wu chi* and *t'ai chi*, since it is such an important one in Taoist thought and one that is so frequently misunderstood. *Wu chi* refers to the Taoist (and Zen) symbol of the Empty Circle and is often viewed as the Empty Void from which Yin and Yang emerged when movement started. This state of movement is symbolized by the famous *t'ai chi* symbol that I reproduced in an earlier chapter. But actually *"wu chi"* does not mean "empty void" as it is so often translated. The Chinese character *"chi"* (not to be confused with the character *"ch'i"* that means "breath" or "vital energy") refers to concepts such as "extreme," "limit," "boundary," or "pole" (in the sense of polarity), while the character *"wu"* means "without" or "empty" in this context.

So *wu chi* more accurately represents the idea of the state of existence before any limits or polarities came into being. A better literal translation would be "the limitless," which is, of course, an alternative way of saying "the infinite." Another way of putting it is to say that *wu chi* is prior to the introduction of any dualities (and therefore before any things at all), which only come into existence with the transition to the polarities and movement expressed within the *t'ai chi*.

The term *"wu chi"* has also been used as another way of referring to the state of consciousness prior to the introduction of any experiential forms, whether they were thoughts or sensory impressions or emotions. It is certainly a description of one of the key states of consciousness sought in meditation. Similarly, as we saw, this was the state of consciousness CXW advised practitioners to stand in before beginning the practice of the *t'ai chi ch'uan* form.

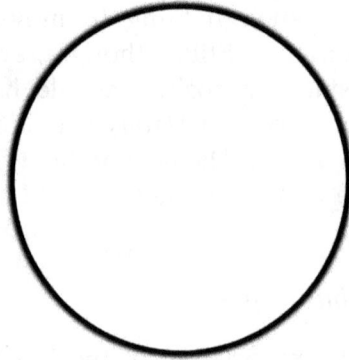

Fig. 14. The Taoist Wu Chi Symbol

In contrast "*t'ai chi*" literally means the "great extremes" or more commonly the "grand ultimate," where Yin and Yang are the two extremes being referenced. This often causes the name of the Chinese martial art *t'ai chi ch'uan*, which is usually translated "grand ultimate boxing," to be similarly misunderstood. This name was not intended to refer to this discipline as the ultimate martial art, as many have supposed. The mistake is that "*t'ai chi*" does not refer to "grand ultimate" but rather to "grand *ultimates*." Accordingly, this title really denotes the fact that this form of boxing is based on the careful discrimination and application of Yin and Yang energies, with movements continuously cycling between different forms of these energies.

At his seminar, CXW gave an interesting demonstration of how the subtle flow of internal *ch'i* energies could be experienced by the novice practitioner. He had us all sit quietly looking to the front of the room while he walked behind us. He then loudly clapped his hands together. At the sound of the clap I felt a faint tingling flutter of energy traversing the back of my neck and down my spine. That feeling, he said, was the *ch'i*. Perhaps my experiences in "The Awakening" described at the beginning of this book and in the "Night Demons" dream were much more intense forms of the flow of this same *ch'i* energy.

12. Vision 4: *The Secret Contract*

Vision Matrix

For Both Sections

Thematic Narrative: Initiation 4 of 5
Session Cluster: 1 of 1
Motif Elements: Sojourn, Dialogue, & TransIdentity

Domain: Etheric

World Level: Surface World
World Realm: Formal
Involvement Level: Passive
Direction of Focus: Centered

Section 1

Subject: Identity, Thinking
Content: Empty

Consciousness: Deep Trance
Participation Mode: Disembodied Witness
Population Level: Populated

Section 2

Subject: Identity, Thinking, Myself, Embodied
Content: Visual

Consciousness: Threshold
Participation Mode: Embodied Witness
Population Level: Empty

Day 3: "The Secret Contract"

While I never retained any memory of entering into a deep trance or *wu chi* state of consciousness, on the third day of meditation I was surprised to find myself coming to awareness on the periphery of one of these states. I was in the fuzzy border region lying between normally veiled states of consciousness and the state I was usually in prior to the onset of visions. This was because I heard in my head the last fragments of a conversation between an unknown party and someone whom I took to be speaking for me.

The voices weren't really "heard" though. They had a nebulous quality that made them seem more like thoughts than spoken words. Since there was no sound, I was unable to associate any distinguishing features such as age or gender with them. Their quality was more like a faint echo. Although I heard fragments from a much longer conversation, I was only able to remember the last pieces of the exchange, as the echoes quickly faded away.

Also absent was the presence of any visual field, including the kind I normally experienced in relaxed Threshold consciousness. It might be more accurate to say that if a visual field was present, I took no notice of it. I did have some faint awareness of my body's presence. It was as if the input from my external senses of sight and sound had been suppressed, but I was still receiving limited signals from the subtler energy vibrations of my physical body.

What I "heard" was what I took to be a surrogate for myself making an agreement with another unidentified party, though I did not remember the details of what preceded it or what had been agreed to. I do recall the outlines of a discussion where I was presented with a list of rules I was expected to follow if I went on some kind of quest, but I have no memory of the specifics. The party whom I took to be me was asked: "Will you agree to do this?" My surrogate's reply was, "Yes, I will." The echoes of this whole exchange so disturbed me that I immediately dropped out of meditational consciousness and returned to normal awareness.

Commentary

I definitely felt at the time that a transaction had taken place and that it concerned me, but I did not understand how that could be. I was somewhat unsettled by the thought that some one had just committed me to a set of behaviors I was neither aware of nor had agreed to. I hoped this spectral self had not signed anything. Where was Daniel Webster from Benét's Faustian tale, "The Devil and Daniel Webster," when you needed him? I had no clues concerning the identity of the other party beyond whatever scant hints were provided by previous visions. I considered the possibility that it was one of the Watchers, though subsequently I learned this was not the case.

There was an additional element to this experience that made it even more puzzling. Although the participant in the conversation identified himself by the first person singular ("Yes, I will") and seemed to be acting as my agent, I had the distinct impression that I was not meant to hear this conversation. This was similar to the feeling I had regarding the incidents with the two Watchers, who behaved as if I was not aware of their presence. I wondered why I always felt like an eavesdropper in my own visions. Was it because they weren't really mine?

One possible explanation was that meditation was giving me limited access into areas of consciousness normally quarantined from me (there's that Chinese wall again). Whether by evolution or design, certain areas of consciousness were purposefully being kept hidden from me. This was not such an outlandish suggestion, since the vast majority of our previous memories and experiences are unavailable to us.

Similarly, my body was constantly engaged in a complex system of automatic processes and drives that impacted my mind that were not accessible to conscious governance. It could be that meditation had inadvertently opened a back door into one of these processes and my mind had created a symbolic narrative for that event in terms I could understand.

Or perhaps my Soul was guiding me towards a revelation by presenting me with these characters purposefully oblivious to my presence.

Are Two I's Better than One?

Neither of these explanations specifically addressed my concern that trance-"I" was agreeing to an unknown undertaking that I, the non-trance-"I," had not. Dr. Freud and his numerous disciples had spent over a century acclimating us to the possibility of multiple components lurking in our unconscious. It was remarkable how comfortable we had become with the concept of unconscious drives pushing our buttons.

But this experience felt distinctly non-Freudian in character. The other "I" did not seem to be just another aspect of a larger self. Instead, similar to the Watchers from the previous days, this "I" felt as if it were a separate autonomous being. And more disturbingly, it acted as if it were the one in control, not my conscious self. In retrospect, I should probably have seen that for the important clue it was.

Whether this character was a figment of my imagination or not, someone or something was engaged in a private undertaking within my person without my knowledge. If that other "I" were the creation of my imagination, then *imagination* was the puppeteer, manipulating the strings on the phantom "I" to tell its story. No matter how I characterized it, whether as another "I", as some Freudian world of the unconscious, or as the imagination, there was an unknown force masquerading as the "I" lurking behind my normal consciousness. And meditation had caught a glimpse of it.

At least two different selves or personas were involved here, one active and aware during regular meditation and the other buried in a hidden realm partially accessible via trance-like states. Was this the Yin self to my Yang one? If Freud were to be believed, this latter self was always present in this deeper layer of consciousness, spinning its webs (the Trickster?) and pushing my buttons.

Another possibility was this was a phenomenon that could only be manifested during trance-like states and would lie dormant until activated, similar to the seed awaiting the right conditions of warmth and rain to push its head up through the dirt into the sunlight.

A third possibility was that my vision of the Self was a tenuously held together construct that would begin to unravel as soon as I subjected it to the inner light of meditation. I hoped that later meditative experiences would help to shed more light on these alternatives.

The Sojourn Motif

The main characteristic of the Sojourn motif, like that of the Vignette one, focuses on the relationship of the observer to the subject matter of the vision. During visions of this type I would find myself "dropping in" on situations in which other actors were engaged in dialogue or in other types of interactions. These actors and the nature of their relationship constituted the primary content of this type of vision. I would not be a party to this interaction, nor would the vision's actors be aware of my presence.

This latter factor distinguishes this motif from that of the Vignette. The Watchers knew I was there, for example, but not that I was aware of them. They were, after all, watching me. This particular case of the Sojourn motif was distinctive, however, for one of the subjects in the situation I dropped into was acting as a surrogate for myself, or at least my conscious self. There was no indication, however, that this persona had any knowledge of my having overheard any of the conversation.

This type of vision would be very similar to the phenomenon called "remote viewing." I would not necessarily recognize any of the parties in the vision or anything about the nature of the situation. I might also recognize I was lacking enough of the background details to understand the situation. To me this vision would come across as if it were a random event, as if somehow the psychic wires had gotten crossed or a conversation had been accidentally overheard. Within this type of vision I might overhear dialogue but not experience any visual elements (as in the present case), or instead have glimpses of scenes of various durations rendered across a wide spectrum of visual detail. In those cases where I did experience visual information, my point of view would remain static.

I would experience this kind of phenomenon quite frequently, though with varying degrees of intensity and resolution. These experiences usually occurred during the beginning of my meditation session and probably have happened hundreds of times since I started the Practice. Hearing voices at some point during meditation was the rule, not the exception.

I should add, lest some form of schizophrenia be suspected, that none of these voices ever told me what to do, except obliquely in the present case. And in this instance I had no clue about what it was I was supposed to do. In fact, I got the distinct impression that in every instance of Sojourns, with the exception of the few I will report on, the conversations I heard had nothing at all to do with me.

For the most part the individuals involved in these Sojourn experiences seemed engaged in their own small private dramas, ones I had somehow stumbled upon accidentally, much as if I had been randomly channel surfing across some psychic network. In most of these, because of their distinctly random feel and limited duration, I rarely formed any lasting memories of their content. As a result, this is not a type of motif for which I will be providing much additional discussion, except in those few cases where I did form significant memories.

The Etheric Domain

This particular vision is very different from those I have previously described, as well as from other examples of this motif I experienced. In the vast majority of my visions there was a well-formed visual field. Objects or individuals were usually present. These kind of visions typically had a distinct foreground and background, ranging from the black formless empty space seen in the "Ghost Guru" vision to the more fully resolved meditation room of the two "Watcher" visions. In this case no visual field of any kind was present, not a black void, not a white void, nothing at all.

It would therefore not be correct to describe this experience as a void or empty space. There was no visual space present at all. Since none of the ordinary dimensions of space were present, perhaps the best way to refer to this absent field was as one of zero-dimensions. In mathematics, zero dimensional space is defined in terms of a point. But a point is still defined in terms of a location in three-dimensional space, albeit one that has no extension. Space would still exist.

What was so unusual about this vision was that the experience of visual space did not exist at all, at least from the point of view of my consciousness. We are very familiar with the phenomenon of an absent visual field based on our everyday experience. It is an experience we are always having whenever our eyes are open. I refer, as you might guess, to the area that exists past the edge of our peripheral vision. We see no border there, no black edge, no empty space. We see nothing at all. That form of nothing was exactly what I saw (or more accurately didn't see) in this vision.

I think the best way to describe this absent form of space would be to call it a null space, a space whose location could only be spoken about in abstract terms within the Formal realm. A variation of the classical concept of Ether would be a good fit from the domain point of view, if we regard the Ether as the dimension that remained once all dimensions of space were removed. Think of this Ether as the region of potential, yet-to-be-actualized space, much like that unseen region now sitting in the twilight zone past the edge of your visual field.

Over the course of my Practice, an increasing number of experiences in Threshold consciousness occurred within the Etheric domain, as the normally vibrating black field behind my eyelids grew more and more transparent over time. This type of unresolvable black expanse is another example of the Etheric domain, since it represents the form of empty space that remains when all normal input to the mind's visual field is suppressed. From the standpoint of Threshold consciousness, it appears as a region of unrealized visual space, the realm where visions from I-Maginal consciousness could potentially take shape.

The "I" of the Storm

The question of where the vast majority of these Sojourn experiences were coming from is a puzzling one. Were they chaff from an overly active imagination accidently breaking through psychic walls weakened by the act of meditation, a kind of psychic effluence? Or, more significantly, were they the result of previously latent psychic powers becoming activated by meditation, giving me glimpses into the remote interactions of other individuals in this or other realms or timelines? My suspicion is that these unknown voices were actually those of different personas of my Soul that were engaged in their own ongoing, autonomous behaviors. These activities were normally hidden from my conscious self, which was usually focused on living its own life. They were buried deep within the realms of the Soul's different Worlds, ones to which I would be given greater access in later stages of the Practice.

As my earlier discussion of this vision indicated, I certainly believed something had taken place that was very different from almost every other Sojourn conversation I had ever heard. Why in this single instance did I believe the voice calling itself "I" was speaking for me? How did I know this wasn't just another utterance from one of the many other speakers I often heard while meditating? Maybe this "I" belonged to one of them; it was not my "I," but someone else's.

The only explanation I can give for my belief is that this experience felt "just so," just like the way a Zen practitioner might put it. I don't know what else I can say. The response of my conscious self (my persona) to hearing that exchange was fundamentally different in kind from its response to all the other overheard exchanges that occurred over the course of the Practice. In this case the voice was speaking for me and as me; in all the other cases the voices belonged to no one I recognized or perhaps to no one at all.

The validation of the presence of another self based on an experience that felt "just so" is significant, because at rock bottom, the sense of self is ultimately just a peculiar kind of feeling, or more accurately, a constellation of feelings and thoughts and memories. It might be a special form of aggregate feeling. But in the end it is just a feeling. And because it is a feeling, it is something that could potentially go away or be suppressed, as was reported to occur in certain deep states of meditation (or mental illness).

A Reader's Quiz to Digest

In order to test my view that the concept of "self" is nothing but a constellation of associated feelings, I've put together this little unscientific quiz. Ask yourself the following kinds of questions:

1. *Do you feel at home in your body?*
2. *Do you feel at home in the world?*
3. *Do you feel in control of the movements of your body?*
4. *Do your perceptions match your memories?*
5. *Do you recognize yourself when you look in the mirror?*
6. *Do you feel distinct from all other things in the world?*
7. *Do you feel you are the source of your thoughts and behaviors?*
8. *Do you have a sense of autonomy and free will?*

If you answered "yes" or "probably" to most of these questions, you very definitely have a self; you identify yourself with your own "I-ing." Notice that I'm not expressing any judgment about whether that's a good thing or not. I'll leave the decision about the value or existence of a personal self to you until after you've been meditating for a while. In particular, you might come to feel a little differently about your answer to the last three questions after spending some time in the unconscious realms as I have, or even after you have finished all three of these books.

Taken together, the point I'm trying to make with this little quiz is that these kinds of meta-feelings constitute the experience of "self." Take away these feelings and your self will disappear, along with your customary view of the world and assumed place in it. A disruption in the integrity of these feelings is probably one of the major causes of many mental disorders, as well as a much sought-after state in certain Buddhist spiritual traditions.

The States of Consciousness

The Deep Trance consciousness is the location where the conversation involving my "other self" occurred. This is distinguished from I-Maginal consciousness, where the vast majority of my visionary experiences took place, and Threshold state of consciousness, the beginning state of meditational consciousness.

Normally no memories were formed of any of the experiences that transpired in this Deep Trance state, unlike the case with other kinds of consciousness, including, of course, everyday (External) consciousness. All of these other states were a potent source of memories, depending upon the vibrancy and vividness of their experiences.

Neuroscientists studying consciousness have established a correspondence between the kinds of states of consciousness occurring in meditation and the brainwave patterns measured by EEG (electroencephalogram) technology when the subjects were in those states. This is very similar to work in sleep science that measured the brain wave patterns associated with different phases of sleep and dreaming.

While EEG technology is somewhat one-dimensional and typically captures only surface level oscillations of electrical signals in the brain, it is a useful tool for exploring the ways in which states of consciousness are organized into discrete spectral levels, similar to the colors of the spectrum. The following table shows the brainwaves typically associated with the various states of consciousness appearing in meditation. During these stages in real life, there would usually be a mixture of brainwaves of various frequencies and clusters. This chart indicates the predominant brainwave pattern normally associated with that state.

Spectra of Meditative Consciousness			
Meditative Stage	*Sleep Stage*	*Brainwave State*	*Oscillations per second*
External	Awake / Dreaming	Beta	13 - 40
Threshold	Stage 1, Light Sleep	Alpha	7 - 13
I-Maginal	Stage 2, Sleep	Theta	4 - 7
Deep Trance	Deep Sleep	Delta	0 - 4

As the practitioner's awareness passes into the deeper stages of meditational consciousness, the frequency of the associated brainwaves becomes increasingly slower. Because of the reciprocal relationship existing between frequency and wavelength, the corresponding wavelengths would also grow longer as well. Metaphorically, meditative consciousness is like a body of water whose surface becomes calmer as the passage of waves grows slower over time. The Alpha, Theta, and Delta brainwave patterns are similarly associated with the sleep stages of Stage 1 light sleep, Stage 2 sleep, and Stage 3 deep sleep. The REM Stage (dreaming) surprisingly exhibits (among other things) the Beta waves seen in the waking state.

While this table deals with brainwaves and frequencies, it says nothing about the relative amplitudes of waveforms in the different states. There is evidence that in certain of the lower frequency states, the amplitude of the waves tends to increase in magnitude. This is known to be the case in the Delta waves of deep sleep, for example. Both frequency and amplitude are relevant factors in determining the richness of the experience brainwaves could express.

If there were an independent awareness that existed in the Deep Trance state, where an observer witnessed and participated in on-going activities and transactions, something about this awareness made it inaccessible to these other more conscious states of awareness. Perhaps the patterns of information represented within the slower frequency brainwaves of Deep Trance consciousness could not be represented within the higher frequency encodings of the more highly resolved states of awareness. They would therefore fall out of phase during the transition from one stage of consciousness to the next.

This is not to say some awareness could not arise within Deep Trance consciousness, but only that it would be different in kind from that experienced in these other states. Maybe that was why the only evidence for the existence of activity within this Deep Trance state that I saw in the Threshold state took the form of low-resolution thought traces, which rapidly faded away even as I tried to capture them. Perhaps my many other experiences with the fleeting visions of the Sojourn motif were likewise the left over echoes of experiences from Deep Trance consciousness.

The Body Politic

Lacking well-formed memories from the Deep Trance state, it is impossible for me to determine whether the surrogate "I" that I momentarily glimpsed was an independent self that lived beneath my conscious self and potentially controlled my behaviors or some other agent from my unconscious that had no significant connection to me. If the former, then potentially it was an autonomous persona, with its own associated set of inner thoughts, images, emotions, motivations, etc. Jung referred to this kind of psychic construction as an "autonomous complex." But without additional evidence about the nature of these complexes, questions about the persistence and coherence of these alternative selves would remain.

Do these hidden selves become activated only when they are perceived within non-trance states of consciousness, similar to the hibernating characters encoded in video games that lie dormant until summoned into existence by the game's narrative, animated by the life-giving cycles of processing power? Or are they instead self-catalyzing processes, ones that are coherent enough to generate their own internal transformations and narratives, even if "nobody" else besides them was watching? These are the kinds of questions that I will need to investigate as I encounter more varied kinds of meditational experiences.

With all these different states of consciousness lurking about, you might think I was beginning to feel a little like a split personality. Most psychologists view multiple selves or autonomous complexes as a bad thing, believing they resulted from a broken and fragmented self, a disease needing to be cured. A healthy personality should always remain intact.

"One central personality is necessary to keep our psychic house in order," they might argue. After all, as Lincoln said, "A house divided against itself cannot stand." This is the conventional wisdom, which perhaps has its roots in the ancient doctrine of monotheism, the belief in one and only one God. There are exceptions, of course, to this dogma, most notably the post-Jungian, James Hillman. But, as Hillman so passionately advocated, maybe the concept of a single self or unitary personality is the real culprit, just as problematic in his mind as the belief in the existence of a single ruler of the universe (Hillman, 1988).

Chinese philosophy also embraced the concept of a person having multiple Souls and Spirits, with certain schools holding that there were seven animal Souls (*p'o*) and three heavenly Souls (*hun*). The seven animal souls were associated with the Seven Emotions: happiness, joy, anger, grief, love, hatred, and desire. These emotions were said to be detrimental to the Taoist process of self-cultivation. The three heavenly Souls were viewed as categories of "spirit energies," and consisted of mind/heart spirit, bright spirit, and immortal spirit, perhaps comparable with some of Wilber's transpersonal forms of consciousness.

In this pantheon of souls and spirits we are not so much a body as we are a "body politic." This is why I personally tend to hold the idiosyncratic view that the many passages in the *Tao-Te-Ching* purporting to discuss good governance are more about how to achieve self-unity and harmony than how to rule a nation state. Consider this passage quoted earlier from Lao Tzu's chapter 10:

"Can you love your people equally?
Make diverse parts a whole?
Find harmony among your members,
Take no action; pursue no goal?"

The "people" in this passage could very well refer to the many different Soul and Spirits entities Lao Tzu believed existed, especially given the first stanza of this chapter:

> *"Can Animal (p'o) and Spiritual (ying) Souls*
> *Be embraced as one in your heart?*
> *Can you hold fast to true unity?*
> *Never let it depart?"*

The good governance interpretation is almost universally accepted for the many passages that seem directed at a country's rulers. There is probably an element of truth to both these interpretations. That would entail that the principles that are best for harmonizing the different elements of the Self are the same ones that the leader should follow in guiding the nation. Lao Tzu sums up his governing philosophy in passages from chapter 57 of the *Tao-Te-Ching*:

> *"Use this principle to order the country…*
> *By minimal effort, gain all under Heaven.*
> *How do we know these things?*
> *By this! …*
> *Therefore, the wise sage says:*
> *I take no action (wu wei),*
> *And the people transform themselves.*
> *I choose serenity,*
> *And the people regulate themselves.*
> *I make no effort,*
> *And the people prosper by themselves.*
> *I have no desire,*
> *And the people become authentic on their own."*

13. Dream 3: *Lost In the Void*

Vision Matrix

For Both Sections

Thematic Narrative: Night Shadows 3 of 3
Session Cluster: 1 of 1

Content: Visual
Domain: Etheric

World Level: Under World
Involvement Level: Passive
Population Level: Empty
Direction of Focus: Centered

Section 1

Motif Elements: Void

Subject: Absent

World Realm: Zero
Consciousness: Deep Trance
Participation Mode: Pure Presence

Section 2

Motif Elements: Ideation

Subject: Identity, Thinking, Myself

World Realm: Formal
Consciousness: I-Maginal
Participation Mode: Disembodied Witness

"Lost In the Void"

To supplement my discussion of Deep Trance consciousness begun in the previous chapter, I will recount one final dream I had about twenty years ago. This dream was significant because it gave me my first glimpse into the types of experiences Deep Trance meditation might provide. Like the previous vision, it also took place in two parts, one blending into another. Looking back, it definitely had the feel of a meditative vision, though one occurring during sleep.

Section 1. The dream occurred within the initial hours of falling asleep. When it began, I was present only as a disembodied spirit inside a black void, much as I was in the "Cosmic Echoes" dream. But in this dream, I had no sense of floating in a vast expanse. There was no visual tableau spread out before me. I felt I was nowhere at all, lost inside a deep, hollow, black emptiness.

The silence was total, but more than that there was a complete lack of any type of vibration stirring. This applied to my body as well. It had vanished, along with all its accompanying senses. I had nothing to see with, nothing to hear with, and nothing to touch with. I could not even say I was just a point of awareness, since there was not enough awareness for even a point to form and nothing to attach awareness to.

Nor did I feel any emotional response to this situation. Emotionally I was as totally empty as I could possibly imagine. I felt no emotions of fear or worry, no sense of wonder or surprise, no feelings of happiness or sadness. I felt nothing. I was nothing. There was no "I."

Somehow, even in this great absence, something of me persisted. How could I be nothing and yet present as pure consciousness? That was the mystery. I still had a sense of being, even without the presence of any thoughts. I was simply pure presence, but a presence built on absence.

Was this sense of empty presence the same as a sense of self? I'm not sure. If it were, then Descartes would have had it all wrong. The "I AM" had no need of thoughts to exist. For one dream moment, I existed purely as the void. The thoughts came, but they came later. Descartes famous pronouncement was, "I think, and therefore I am." But I believe the correct version of Descartes' revelation should read, "I am, and therefore I think." Or, perhaps more correctly, "Presence, followed sometime later by Thinking."

Section 2. The thoughts, when they came, took an odd turn. Rather than wondering where I was or what was happening, I was already aware of being in this strange state of consciousness. I seemed to know who I was. My only concern was focused on the state of my being. My first thought was, "Maybe this is what it feels like to be dead. Wait! Am I dead? Well, no, probably not. But maybe if I am, it's not so bad. No feelings, no emotions, no worries. Just an eerie sense of silent peacefulness."

I sent my mind out into the surrounding void to see if I could detect anything at all, but there was truly nothing there. I wondered if the peacefulness I was feeling was what remained when all other feelings and emotions and sensations had gone. I don't remember how this dream ended. I must have awakened from this dream in order to form the vivid memories I have of it, but if I did, I immediately fell back to sleep. I have no recollection of having woken up.

Commentary

Looking back on this dream-like event, I believe it was actually a form of meditative experience. It is true that in the immediate aftermath of this event, the possibility I had experienced a form of meditative vision did not occur to me, since at that time I had no experience with that kind of consciousness. Instead I took it to be an imagined enactment of the death experience provided by some unconscious force, one sent perhaps to assuage a lurking fear of death. It is only now in the midst of writing this book that this event appears to me in a very different light.

Certain Hindu philosophies held that the deepest state of sleep was identical to the highest type of meditative consciousness, an empty state found in Deep Trance consciousness, but one in which the most experienced yogis could still maintain an awareness. Wilber, for example, in one of his journals writes about an experience in which he remained aware during deep sleep over a period of several nights.

Maybe I hadn't experienced a dream at all, but instead had accidently discovered another pathway into Deep Trance consciousness that occurred while I was asleep. If so, maybe that's why I was able to remember this visionary type of experience in contrast to the vast majority of everyday dreams. The latter are destined to remain forgotten because they are not vivid enough to trigger the formation of memories.

On the other hand, if this wasn't a meditative experience, had I instead merely dreamt of being in a deep meditative state while in a REM dream? But was there really a difference between the two? The Taoist philosopher Chuang Tzu addresses this issue in a famous dream passage:

> "Once Chuang Chou dreamt he was a butterfly, a butterfly flitting and fluttering around, happy with himself and doing as he pleased. He didn't know he was Chuang Chou. Suddenly he woke up and there he was, solid and unmistakable Chuang Chou. But he didn't know if he was Chuang Chou who had dreamt he was a butterfly, or a butterfly dreaming he was Chuang Chou. Between Chuang Chou and a butterfly there must be some distinction! This is called the Transformation of Things." (Chuang-Tzu 1964, p. 45).

The question of whether I was in a meditative state or merely dreaming I was in a meditative state is one of those kinds of questions that might be completely nonsensical, similar to the dilemma Chuang Tzu expressed in the tale of his butterfly dream. Or, it might be one of those mysteries that could only be solved in the light of deeper experiences within meditative practice. Not surprisingly, the butterfly is in many traditions a symbol for the soul.

But even then, of course, the question regarding the authenticity of the meditative experience might always remain, unless something about the quality of the experience carried with it its own self-authentication, in the same way as a tautology embodies the conditions of its own truth.

The Void Motif

Even though I did not realize it at the time, this dream, which falls under the Void motif, provided my first glimpse of what the Deep Trance state of meditational consciousness might be like. This experience predated by quite a lot my first taste of Deep Trance during the Practice, which I described earlier in the "Secret Contract" vision. In that vision, though, I glimpsed more of what I would call a fading echo of that state rather than a genuine immersion in it. My experience of that echo took place from my perspective as a Disembodied Witness, which was a very different type of consciousness than the one I was in during the dream.

One way to identify a truly immersive experience within Deep Trance would involve the recognition of the type of consciousness I introduced here as Pure Presence. Pure Presence is very similar to the Buddhist concept of Witness, which is one possible answer to the Zen riddle, "Who is having these experiences?" But it is a more fundamental and primordial concept.

Based on my experiences, I would say Pure Presence is all that remains once all other components are subtracted from consciousness. When there is no I-Maginal content or sensory data, no thoughts, no body, no emotions, no memories, no self, and all that is left within consciousness is a featureless black void, that black void *is* the Pure Presence. Strictly speaking, I wasn't able to identify Pure Presence as active in this experience until I was conscious within Section 2 of the vision, since in Section 1 there was nothing present to be witnessed beyond Pure Presence's experience of itself. Pure Presence *just was the simple awareness of its own emptiness.*

The Western reader will no doubt be troubled by the paradoxical nature of that last statement. But the Taoist would not be. For this was not "emptiness" in the usual sense of the word. It was emptiness that itself contained a presence, a presence that was its own empty awareness. Although this empty awareness was preliminary to an actual thought, it was in essence the primordial seed of thought. Using the principle I employed earlier, I would say that it represented the potential clearing in which thought and all other components of consciousness could arise.

Although I resisted the use of the point concept in the case of my discussion of the nonexistent visual space in the "Secret Contract" vision, I do view this type of thought as a *Point thought.* While it represented a presence within the black void, it was one that had no content and no extension. It was a point, but one *prior* to a point of view.

In mathematics, a point is the smallest mathematical entity that can exist. It is so small that a line segment contains an infinite number of them. But now imagine instead you are inside the point; you are in fact its very consciousness. What would that be like? I submit that the experience would be precisely the one that occurred within this dream, the primordial consciousness of Pure Presence. All that would be present would be this endless black void. I say endless because no boundaries could ever exist, since there were no dimensions to this space. Like the Tao is often described, it would be both the smallest of things and the largest of things. According to Lao Tzu in chapter 14, the Tao

> *"… is known as the form of the formless,*
> *The image of the no-thing.*
> *It is called the 'elusive,' the 'mysterious.'*
> *Face it; its front will not be visible.*
> *Follow it; its back will not be visible.*
> *Hold onto the timeless Tao*
> *To master the present moment.*
> *The ability to know its timeless beginning*
> *Is called the 'thread of the Tao.'"*

The Etheric Domain: Where was No-Where?

This vision contained another example of the Etheric domain referred to earlier in the "Secret Contract" vision. I have always been puzzled about why so many spiritual traditions view the realm in which nothing at all was experienced as representative of a higher level of consciousness. To me it seems the opposite. But maybe this realm represents something more substantial than just the primordial state of consciousness that is prior to the introduction of any sensation or thought.

In particular, maybe what I was experiencing was instead an important boundary demarcating different realms of consciousness. Maybe it was an abyss that separated human forms of consciousness from those belonging to beings of higher and more transcendent spirituality. It would act as a barrier, a region of emptiness that had to be crossed before the practitioner could access higher realms. Perhaps such realms could only be reached once the practitioner had completed numerous kinds of quests across multiple spiritual levels, like the ones Wilber described in his account of the transpersonal levels.

Or maybe, this realm might not have been the Etheric domain it appeared to be at all. Perhaps it only appeared empty and hollow because I had not yet developed the inner faculties required for perceiving what really existed in this domain. Like the newborn infant, I had yet to learn how to see.

The Zero Realm: Making Something out of No-Thing

Although it might appear so, this realm was not an example of what you might want to call the Null realm. It is true that it didn't make sense to talk about the resolution of this realm, since there wasn't any content accessible. But there was a featureless black void, and some degree of visual content was present, namely the absence of any other content. The all-encompassing darkness was this absence.

Accordingly, rather than being an example of the Null realm, this is a pure case of the Zero realm. The defining characteristic of this Zero realm is that there is no content available to be experienced beyond the primordial awareness of presence within an empty featureless space. The only sensation that could be perceived in this realm would be the total lack of all sensations. The diffuse sensation of an all encompassing, tranquil peacefulness was something that only appeared following the transition to I-Maginal consciousness, where the sensation was created in response to the lingering echoes of the prior realm.

Once any type of sensation or thought appeared within this featureless arena, the experience would move from the Zero realm to the Ideation motif of the Formal realm. Thoughts and ideas would be the only content present in this realm. While there might be indistinct and unformed elements of other kinds of content inhabiting the background of the Formal realm, its presence would be experienced more as noise or distraction rather than as independent components contributing to the content of the vision.

An important characteristic of the Void motif was that its recollection would always involve a transition from the Zero to the Formal realms. In these transitions Pure Presence would transform to become some form of Witness, whether Pure, Disembodied or Embodied, and consciousness would move from the Deep Trance state into I-Maginal or Threshold ones. Without my transitioning from these deeper states into at least some rudimentary level of awareness, these states would remain totally hidden and outside the range of experience. That is why any visionary experience of Pure Presence within the Void motif would always lead to these transitional states. A similar but much more traumatic phenomenon perhaps occurs in the case of night terrors, which appear during periods of sudden arousal from deep Delta wave sleep.

Swimming in the Deep

During my first week of meditation, I had certain experiences suggestive of these Deep Trance states. Typically, after about ten minutes within Threshold consciousness, while my body started to relax and grow numb, I would enter into a state of consciousness absent of all awareness. The transition into this state of non-awareness could be described, using video editing vernacular, as an abrupt cut, since no memories of this transition remained.

When I came out of this state, which would normally take another ten minutes, I would have no recollection of having entered into it or what had transpired while I was there. At most I might experience lingering echoes or traces of images from what would have been the state of Deep Trance consciousness. This would occur if the movement back into Threshold consciousness was not abrupt but more of an overlapped blending between the two.

Since I typically spent some amount of time during meditation in periods of non-consciousness, as I did, of course, during sleep, it is quite possible some portion of this period was spent in deeper states of consciousness. Deep Sleep and Deep Trance meditational consciousness are very similar from a brainwave frequency point of view, since both display very slow delta waves.

The fact I had no awareness from my time spent in these states of consciousness showed my mind's inability to form any memories from this period without my first returning to a more aware state of consciousness, as would be indicated by the presence of higher frequency brain waves. A similar phenomenon occurs with the vast majority of dreams in REM sleep, but also perhaps among some of the visions occurring in I-Maginal consciousness. In those occasions I would not be able to recall my experiences because I would have failed to successfully transition to more active states of consciousness before my memory of them totally faded.

14. Vision 5: *Tunneling towards the Light*

Vision Matrix

Thematic Narrative: Initiation 5 of 5
Session Cluster: 1 of 1
Motif Elements: Exit, Traversal, Portal, & Tunnel

Subject: Identity, Thinking, Myself, Embodied
Content: Visual, Depth, Animated, Navigated
Domain: Etheric, Symbolic

World Level: Surface World
World Realm: Formal
Participation Mode: Embodied Witness
Involvement Level: Passive
Population Level: Solitary
Direction of Focus: Centered
Consciousness: Threshold

Day 6: "Tunneling towards the Light"

On this day (New Year's Day) I found myself once more returning to Threshold consciousness after an unspecified period of non-consciousness during my meditational Practice. For part of the time I may have been in Deep Trance consciousness. According to my normal practice during Threshold consciousness, I focused my attention on the slowly drifting amorphous shapes appearing within my darkened visual field. After a little time had passed, I noticed the pattern of movement within the field was undergoing a transformation.

Where previously there had been random patterns of large blotches of dark colors, a more homogeneous image was forming. The shapes had become much smaller and more numerous, but at the same time fairly uniform in size, shape, color and distribution across the field.

Imagine the pattern of white static that used to appear on analogue televisions when they were tuned to a non-broadcasting channel (like in the movie *Poltergeist*, for example). Now invert the image, so that black became white and white black, and do a similar inversion for the in-between values. That was how the image in my visual field appeared. It also had the same electric dynamism that static had, with the grainy dark shapes vibrating and flickering in and out. I was still in Threshold consciousness. Was my mind looking for a channel to tune into?

This pattern continued for what seemed like a couple of minutes, and then began to change again. A small spherical black shape started to form in the middle of the visual field, surrounded by a brighter halo of pulsating energy. It quickly stabilized in size and stopped growing. If I imagined the size of my visual field to be that of an 8 1/2 x 11 inch sheet of paper, the black hole would have been about the size of a dime placed in its center.

The black hole was not flat but appeared as a three-dimensional pulsating sphere, similar to the inverted after-image of an agitated sun. Short segments of thin rectangular shapes radiated out from all sides of the sphere. These segments did not touch the central sphere but floated outside it, forming a ring of rays, much like a child might draw in a picture of the sun. There were approximately 24 rays surrounding the central image.

This ring was not static but gradually increasing in diameter, moving away from the center as it grew. As one ring of segmented rays left its orbital, another of its previous size immediately replaced it. From my perspective, a series of concentric moving rings of rays were constantly pulsating out from the center mass, moving towards me and past me, and ultimately disappearing as they left my field of view.

There were two different ways for me to process what I was seeing. On the one hand, there was an image of a pulsating, sun-like orb, sending rows of concentric rays out from its center. That was how I initially experienced this phenomenon. This assumed my point of view was static.

But what if my point of view was not static? Then, instead of looking at a stationary orb hanging in space, I would be traveling down a very long tunnel of energy towards a vibrating source of energy at the open end of the tunnel. The rays that were flowing past me on all sides would be how the walls of the tunnel would appear as I sped past them towards the "light at the end of the tunnel."

Because the tunnel was so long, the size of the open end would not begin to grow until I had travelled for an extended period of time into its interior. Optical illusion or not, this was how I came to view what was happening within my visual field.

As I continued to focus on this image, it began to transform again. At the north-south and east-west poles of the center orb at a distance a couple diameters out from the orb, there began to form ancillary circular regions, which gently pulsed in size and intensity. They were about a quarter of the size of the central orb.

The feeling of traveling through a tunnel stopped and was replaced by the image of the pulsing dark sun with streaming rays, which were now passing through these four surrounding moon-like areas. Other symmetrical groups of still smaller orbs took the place of additional segments of streaming rays, distributing themselves around the central mass at varying orbitals.

Initially, I felt like I was looking at a pulsating giant black snowflake. But as the images became even more dynamic, with different groupings of symmetrical patterns appearing and disappearing, it was more like I was watching an animated kaleidoscopic display.

The image underwent one last series of transformations. The various distinct elements within each orbital began to coalesce, creating a series of concentric glowing bands of light around the central mass. As this consolidation occurred, the movement of rays out from the center stopped and the bands started to move inward toward the center mass, as if attracted by its gravity. The bands themselves morphed into glowing spheres of energy that grew smaller and smaller as they moved towards the center and eventually vanished.

It appeared as if balls of energy were being flung into my visual field from behind and through my point of view, one after another, shrinking in size as they travelled deeper into the dark space before they finally disappeared. After a little while the progression of new spheres slowed and faded away. My visual field once again became a homogenous static-like area.

At this point a slit of light appeared horizontally across the center of my viewpoint, covering about three quarters of its width. It began to grow larger in the center across its vertical dimension, forming an ovoid shape, similar to a whitish football slowly inflating on its side. In the center of the region a darker area once again began to appear with a pulsating texture like that of the original central orb.

As the slit grew wider more details slowly revealed themselves. More of the dark mass in the center of the ovoid became visible, until its final shape was apparent. It was a variegated dark round area with a black hole in its middle. On either side of it were the tails of the white ovoid shape. I now recognized the whole figure for what it was. It was an eye, filling most of my visual field, now fully open, and looking right at me. It continued to stare at me for a few moments and then faded away, consumed by the shimmering grainy surface of the background energy.

Commentary

In retrospect, what was most unusual about this experience was that it did not occur in a dream or visionary state, but while I was still in Threshold consciousness. I was fully aware both of my surroundings and my body and was engaged in a process of reflection about the meaning of what I was seeing. If this were a hallucination, it was one with its own distinct mode of internal logic fueling its successive transformations.

This experience reflected a new form of awareness different from what I had previously experienced. It might be related to the Zen concept of no-mind. Zen no-mind represented an activity of total engagement, one free from contamination by irrelevant thoughts and emotions. It was a type of tunnel vision in which the only experiences present in consciousness were those necessary for the activity underway. No-mind was similar to the Taoist principle of non-action, but represented a different kind of concentrated attention than the Taoist principle.

Rather than view this form of consciousness as one absent of all thoughts, this type of activity actually required a concentrated, laser- like focus, a kind of *focal thought*. This was an experience that resulted from a highly focused concentration upon the elements of the dark visual field projected behind my closed eyelids. The images I saw were the product of my intense immersion in my experience of them. The energy from my internal gaze catalyzed the genesis of their transformation, one self-sustaining enough not to dissipate under the gaze of my observation, as so many of my other visions had done.

The Traversal Motif

The defining characteristic of the Traversal motif is its symbolic depiction of travel down some form of passageway or interface into a potentially new and unexplored realm. In this vision the opening of a symbolic eye after traveling down an animated tunnel represented for me the possibility that my visionary journey was about to enter a new phase or dimension. The Traversal motif typically appears at the end of one thematic narrative and sometimes at the beginning of a new one. It indicates a new narrative is about to begin, usually taking place within a different realm.

In terms of the elements associated with this motif, I would usually experience this kind of vision as a passive observer. While my point of view might typically be experienced as though I were travelling down some tunnel or passage, sometimes, as in the present case, my orientation within the scene would remain frozen, as if the elements of the scene were moving past me rather than I through them. In either case I would always see some movement occurring within the scene before me.

Because of the abstract nature of this particular experience, it belongs in the Formal realm, within the Symbolic domain. While all visions within meditation are symbolic to some degree or another, and may be assumed to be representative of more than they reveal on their surface, this particular classification level specifically refers to content manifesting a special sense of "symbol."

Symbolic content specifically involves a simple stand-alone shape or integrated configuration of shapes perceived as a whole, one expressing a single, unitary idea or concept. This vision is a strong example of this kind of domain, since it literally represents the concept of "tunnel vision." In the Symbolic domain, no other objects or shapes would be present within the scene, in order to emphasize the specifically symbolic nature of its content. The background, if present at all, would only be visible to the extent it served to push the symbolic form into the foreground.

Water World

Writing about this episode brings to mind another hallucinatory experience I had while experimenting with a Zen style of focused meditation, one that has proven repeatable. While sitting outside on a park bench a couple of months ago, I decided to try an experiment in Zen meditation. I relaxed my body, rested my hands palm up on my thighs, and with my eyes open, stared intensely at the ground in front of me. After just a few minutes, the surface of the ground started to shimmer and distort, as if waves of energy were moving through it. The ground seemed to lose its solidity and become fluid-like with ripples moving across it.

I felt I was transgressing on a dark secret best kept hidden from normal sight. The apparent solidity of the world was a grand illusion, one that would quickly melt away if you looked at it too closely. This was something quantum physicists knew all too well. The fact that the world we perceive is only a projection of our mind is something we also know but tend to forget. I closed my eyes for a second and then reopened them. The world had not regained its solidity. Only when I broke my gaze did the effect disappear.

This experience and others like it led me to formulate a hypothesis about how the location of a point of view impacted the quality of the thing observed. There was a famous experiment in quantum mechanics that illustrated this hypothesis. In the so-called double-slit experiment, a beam of light was directed at two adjacent slits in an opaque board and projected onto a photographic screen behind it. When the beam was not interfered with, and the experiment was observed from the outside, a series of continuous bands of varying intensity would appear on the screen, as if waves of liquid light had caused an interference pattern to emerge.

On the other hand, when measurement devices were added in front of the slits, to record when light passed through them, separate bands indicating the collisions of distinct particles appeared on the screen, as if the light were a collection of particles being shot at the slits. This happened when the phenomena were being observed from the inside of the event.

The conclusion I drew from this was when a phenomenon was observed from outside, as, for example, when a spider hovered above its web with sunlight shimmering on it, the thing observed would take on a wave-like appearance, showing liquid ripples and wave interference patterns. On the other hand, when the phenomenon was observed from the inside, as when the fly saw the spider walking towards it across the web, things would take on a distinctly solid form and appear as discrete entities.

This was what occurred on the bench while I was in the hybrid state of Threshold consciousness. My intense gaze upon the ground, during which I blocked out all other sensory input from sources surrounding me, essentially isolated me from the scene I was observing. I was no longer in the scene. My state of mind in Threshold consciousness had placed me outside it. That was why the solidity of the scene began to dissolve and become more wave-like, along with my sense of self. Once I had let my focus waver and sensations entered my awareness from all sides around me, I was once again embedded within the scene and everything became solid and discrete, including my self, dropping me now into everyday external consciousness.

This could also explain the tunnel vision I had just described. If my immersion in the meditative state had grown deep enough to isolate me from the internal scene I was observing, then the scene should become more wavelike, displaying energy like ripples and wave interference patterns.

I was reminded of the kinds of patterns I had seen on the surface of the water of a shallow swimming pool in bright sunlight, with the shadows of the waveforms bouncing off the bottom of the pool and reflecting back onto the surface. By perturbing the water from beneath with each of my two hands, I was able to create various kinds of wave interference patterns I now realize were very similar to the kinds of patterns I saw this day in meditation. These included the sun-like pattern with the radiating rays, the kaleidoscopic patterns of spheres, and the series of shrinking spheres. The eye looking back at me, of course, was another matter.

Several other kinds of patterns like the ones appearing here also came to mind. The kaleidoscopic images, for example, especially reminded me of photographs of individual snowflakes I had recently seen on the web (Google "snowflake photographs" to see these). The rings of moving orbs I experienced in my vision were very similar to photos of molecular structure (such as of platinum atoms) captured through a field ion microscope, which were distinguished by their arrays of concentric rings.

More relevant to the practice of meditation were the different representations of mandalas created by Tibetan monks. I wondered if the Tibetan monks sitting in meditation had seen mandala-like images as part of their practice and, if so, had developed the ability over time to visualize the extensive and elaborate designs they were so famous for drawing.

Fig. 15. An Example of a Mandala

Holograms and Consciousness

Some of the less resolved images I saw in Threshold consciousness looked remarkably like the grainy two-dimensional recordings of holographic scenes I had seen. Raw holographic images look nothing at all like the objects they represent.

The fact that there was a striking similarity between the wave-like energy patterns I've seen within the darkened visual field during eye-closed meditation and the two-dimensional recordings of three-dimensional holographic scenes has led me to the following conjecture. What if the dynamic energy patterns in my visual field normally appearing in Threshold consciousness were themselves the animated holographic representations of on-going activity within the Worlds of the Soul, ones not yet projected into visionary awareness within I-Maginal consciousness?

Only when my mind achieved the I-Maginal state of consciousness would these visions be fleshed out and presented to awareness. Prior to my mind becoming active in I-Maginal consciousness, these energy patterns would represent the raw unprocessed data of potential visions. This data would be the surface level, two-dimensional representation of the dynamic imagery of a potential visionary scene and would require transformation within I-Maginal consciousness before it could be projected into full, three-dimensional visionary awareness.

This conjecture assumed the narratives expressive of the Soul's activity were self-contained and ongoing, even if they had not yet been experienced in I-Maginal consciousness. This does not imply that the events occurring within these hidden narratives were not being experienced in some form by conscious entities whose activities these narrative chronicled, but only that I, as the conscious persona, had not yet been able to experience them.

Suppose in my meditative experiences I observed situations in which I bounced back and forth between Threshold and I-Maginal consciousness states. If I found myself repeatedly returning to a coherent narrative vision with plot points separated only by gaps in time, that would be evidence of this form of persistence. I have in fact had this type of experience multiple times. While the gaps experienced within Threshold consciousness were typically minutes in duration, I also experienced this same phenomenon of narrative continuity occurring across separate meditative sessions, some of which were separated by periods of weeks.

I have also determined that the kinds of rippling waveform patterns that overlaid and distorted everyday scenes in the Zen open eye experiments were identical in form and pattern to those that appeared when I closed my eyes within the dark visual field and then opened them again. In other words, during Zen Threshold consciousness, the same waveform patterns persisted whether the eyes were closed or open. My theory is that these waveform patterns represented the structured holographic information content of potential experiences, ones accessible within I-Maginal consciousness. In the Zen case, however, these waveforms represented the experiences of everyday reality that would return when normal conscious processing resumed.

In the *Tao-Te-Ching*, several passages refer to the Tao as water-like. In chapter 8, for example, the sage's mind is described as the "*good deep water.*" In chapter 15, which lists several qualities of Tao-like consciousness, the sage's awareness is "*dissolving, like ice beginning to melt*" and "*chaotic, like murky water.*" Chapter 21 has a description of entering into the experiences created by Taoist yoga:

> *"You can enter the cave where power abides.*
> *To do so you must follow the Tao.*
> *There, the Tao will create entities.*
> *They will appear in a blinding flash,*

They will disappear into dim darkness.
Blinding flash (huang)! Dim darkness (hu)!
An Image (hsiang) will appear in its center.
Dim darkness! Blinding flash!
A Being (wu) will appear in its center.
Buried! Obscure!
A Life Seed (ching) will appear in its center.
The Seed will be very real (chen).
An Essence (hsin) will appear in its center.
From antiquity until now
Its name will never go away
So that we may always know
The origin of the many.
How do I know about
The state of the origins of the many?
By This!"

This is another example of a passage that provides descriptions of visionary experiences very similar to ones I have had. In particular, I have had the explicit visionary experience of the "*dim darkness, blinding flash*" phenomenon while in Threshold consciousness. Much of this passage describes the manner in which experiences at one level of consciousness would appear while transitioning into a deeper layer, such as when going from Threshold to I-Maginal consciousness.

The Eye in the Mirror

Having read mystical texts I was naturally familiar with the concept of the third eye, which when opened was said to provide the practitioner with the ability to see into realms beyond those available to normal vision. It was said to be located behind the center of the forehead. In the Hindu tradition it was known as the "brow chakra," or "*ajna*," which was the sixth primary chakra.

Chakras are viewed as the energy junctions within the *subtle* or *energy* body and the meeting points of energy channels, similar to concepts in Chinese acupuncture, in which the life force (*prana*) or vital energies (*ch'i* in Taoist philosophy) moved. The third eye is normally depicted visually as a physical formation on the outside of the forehead, sometimes even literally as a third eye, other times in a more symbolic form.

121

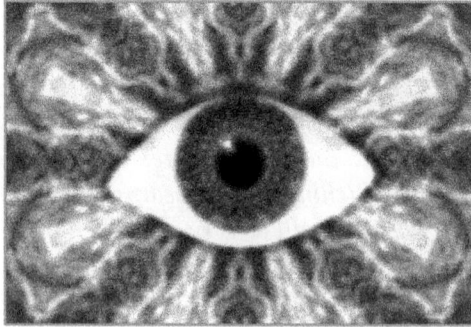

Fig. 16. A Rendering of the Third Eye

What I saw was, of course, inside my head, not outside. I did not have a vision of myself sitting in meditation with a third eye appearing on my forehead. What I saw was an eye that opened and looked right back at me. Whose eye was it? Was it the eye of a spirit watching my mind internally engaged in meditation, much as the two visitors from my earlier visions had observed me from the outside? Or was it a depiction of my own inner eye having opened and now ready to see into other realms? Using the concept of the Witness, maybe this was the figurative representation of the Eye of the Witness.

The latter would be the case if the black visual space I stared into was a dark, liquid, mirror-like surface that reflected back at me my own internal countenance. If so, I would be looking at myself as a structured pattern of internal energy reflected in the Dark Mirror (*hsuan lan*) mentioned in the passage quoted earlier from chapter 10 of the *Tao-Te-Ching*. This reflecting mirror would symbolically represent a portal through which I must pass in order to enter new realms.

Since this vision appeared within the mode of Threshold consciousness, one not very far removed from normal everyday awareness, it represented a new and powerful development in my Practice. It portended the arrival of new kinds of experiences and visions waiting in the deeper, more fertile fields of I-Maginal consciousness.

15. The Initiation Week

The Persistence of Identity

No Matter Where You Go, There You Are

Compared with the wide range of experiences that unfolded over the next many months, those of the first week of the Practice, unusual as they might have seemed at the time, now feel much less significant to me. They feel more like a gentle introduction intended to initiate me, the new practitioner, into the mysteries of the strange realms I was about to visit.

What was most distinctive about the experiences of the first week was the fact that all of them were from the perspective of my normal everyday persona, the so-called ego, albeit one that found itself in somewhat unusual circumstances. The saying "No matter where you go, there you are" certainly applied to me here, at least with respect to that first week.

A quick review of the experiences from that week might help clarify this point. In the case of the "Ghost Guru," even though I did not feel myself physically present, I reflected on what I was seeing with both my identity and memory intact. In particular, I scanned my memory to determine if this was a picture of a younger version of myself or of someone else I might recognize.

In the two instances in which the Watchers visited me, both times I felt myself to be present in the room in which I was sitting. The first day I believed myself to be physically present in the room with them, while on the second I directed my attention onto them without actually feeling I was moving my body. As in the previous case, I scanned my memory to see if I recognized them and did note to myself that while one of the Watchers did resemble a younger version of myself, he was not me but another individual whom I thought I might meet in the future.

The event of the "Secret Contract" was a somewhat more complex situation, insofar as there seemed to be two different versions of me involved. The first was the self who was verbally agreeing to some unknown request by an unknown agent. The other was the self who overheard the last segments of this conversation while sitting in meditation. This second self was, of course, me (my persona). While the first self was not acting under my control, I still recognized it as part of myself. The "Tunneling toward the Light" experience similarly occurred when I, as myself, was sitting in meditation, actively reflecting about what I was seeing.

These latter two events, unlike those of the first two days, all took place within the Threshold state of consciousness. This state, by definition, always involved the presence of a normal "I," one who was usually, but not always, sitting in meditation, but one who was always present within a physical body. The first three meditative experiences, although they took place within deeper states of consciousness, still apparently involved the participation of my normal persona, sometimes with the illusion of having a body and other times not.

The Dream Experience

Was it so surprising that even within the meditative visions taking place in I-Maginal consciousness I would still be present as myself, with my memories, dispositions and ways of thinking about things still intact? After all, even though I didn't have a very large sample of meditative visions to go by after one week, I still had hundreds and maybe thousands of dream experiences to consider as evidence on the question of the persistence of the "I" within non-ordinary consciousness. No matter how diverse or confused or bizarre my dream experiences might have been, the one thing I can say about all of them is that some version of my normal "I" or persona was involved in each and every one of them.

When I speak of dream experiences, of course, I am only speaking about those I remember to some degree, usually because I awoke immediately after having them. This would be an example of the type of blended phase transition I described earlier, which in this case would result from an overlap of experiences between different states of consciousness. These dreams probably only represented a small minority of all those I have had in my life. I have no way of knowing whether those others were similar or completely different in character from the ones I remembered. Maybe the fact that only some were remembered was precisely because of some special quality they possessed that triggered my awakening and subsequent recall of them.

Besides involving some version of my self as their main character, these remembered dreams also had some other attributes commonly associated with the act of dreaming. Usually, the dreams told a story that involved transitioning from one scene to another. Other people were almost always involved, many whom I might have known at some point in my life, while others were fictitious or composite characters. Often the locales were versions of places I had lived or worked or gone to school or traveled to, other times they were composites of places I had seen on TV or in the movies or read about in books.

Even though the dreams might have seemed coherent at the time, in retrospect they were usually a confused conglomerate of people and places from multiple time periods in my life within situations both mundane and fantastical. My own age would vary as well, sometimes I would be younger and other times I would envision myself as much older. Along with my age, my body image would similarly vary; sometimes I would be healthy and fit, other times in various degrees of malady or distress.

Whatever the situation in the dream, I would usually be having thoughts within the dream, usually about what was happening to me within the context of the dream. In addition to having thoughts, even though my body was only an imaginary construction within the dream, my feelings and emotions would be actively engaged, usually tied to the types of thoughts I was having at the time. I would experience basic physical feelings, such as pleasure or discomfort, as well as higher order emotions, often of the more negative variety, such as stress, anxiety, and insecurity. Sometimes I would even experience the physical sensations of an adrenalin rush brought on by the fearful events of the dream.

What's Different about Visions

Losing My Identity

While a persistent sense of identity was present in both my meditative experiences of the first week and my catalogue of dream experiences, this was not always going to be the case among the visions I experienced over the several months following this first week and continuing through the initial stages of writing this book.

Sometimes I would be some version of my self, as in dreams. Other times I would be a completely different person, maybe one of the opposite sex or of a different race, and often I would be no one at all but instead a pure, disembodied spectator. This non-persistence of identity was to be a distinguishing characteristic of the meditative visions I experienced after the first couple of weeks of the practice. This was to be especially true after I had left the Home realm within the Human domain.

Another way in which the experiences of the first week were to differ from those that subsequently followed concerned the setting in which the visions took place. I always experienced my initial visions as my normal self, within the comfortable confines of my own room, where I was sitting in meditation.

Although my initial vision of the "Ghost Guru" appeared within the black void of an empty internal space, it was followed soon after by the first encounter with the two "Watchers" that unfolded in a imaginary and somewhat distorted version of my room as seen from the perspective of where I was sitting. The same was true for the second visit from the "Watchers" that occurred on the next day. The "Tunneling toward the Light" experience took place within Threshold consciousness, where I was comfortably ensconced within my meditation chair. The "Secret Contract" was a somewhat more complex case, since it apparently began hidden within Deep Trance consciousness only to have fragments of it echo into Threshold consciousness.

Losing My Emotions

There was one feature of my meditative visions present in the first week that would continue throughout my Practice. It was also one that would consistently differentiate the experiences of meditative consciousness from those of dream consciousness. No matter how bizarre the situation in which I found myself during a meditative vision, no matter who or what I was, no matter how frightening or disorienting the situation might have been in real life, I never experienced any feeling or normal emotional reaction. Any physical sensations that were normally associated with the presence of strong feelings or emotions were completely absent.

The experience was like I had left my physical body completely and was travelling in realms in which feelings or sensations from my body could no longer reach me. This is not to say that some type of feeling-based response would never occur. Rather, if it did, it would appear as a kind of abstract concern only, one lacking real emotional feeling or associated physical sensations.

This complete lack of emotional feeling was a key element of my meditative visions, no matter from which state of consciousness the visions might have originated. Indeed, if while asleep I experienced a vision devoid of any feeling or emotional content, I would assert that this vision was in fact not one originating in Dream consciousness but instead in I-Maginal or Deep Trance consciousness.

Good examples of these types of vision would be the two I discussed in the previous chapters, those of the "Cosmic Echoes" and "Lost In the Void" dreams. As I suggested above, the sense of "losing the body" may be a key element characteristic of the meditative vision. This does not mean that I would necessarily lack an imagined body in a meditative vision, but rather that I would lack the kinds of sensations and feelings normally associated with having a physical body.

The Thematic Narrative

Because of the similarities of identity, setting, and thematic elements, this group of visions constitutes a thematic narrative. I call this grouping the "Initiation Narrative," since all the visions in the first week, having oriented me to the nature of the visionary experience within meditation, were preparing me for what was to come.

By presenting me with a sampling of several of the different ways meditative experiences could appear, all within the familiar surroundings of my meditation room, these visions helped desensitize me to the potentially disorienting nature of these experiences. At the same time the nature of the sequence of the visions revealed to me something about the way in which different kinds of motifs combine together to form a coherent thematic narrative.

My very first vision introduced me to the disembodied experience of the black void. While the identity of the figure within the photograph carried its own message of content, the vertical shape of the photograph could also symbolize a type of doorway through which I would pass to begin my travels. The vision of the tunnel and the opening eye at the end of the week similarly indicated the end of one journey and the gateway into another realm. At the same time it showed me how I could have visionary experiences even while within the Threshold state of consciousness.

The two related Watcher visions and the experience of the other-I in the "Secret Contract" represented the central theme of this narrative, which involved me beginning the discipline of meditational sitting and receiving some encouragement, along with a set of guidelines about how I should proceed in the Practice. They also introduced me to additional forms my visions could take, with the embodied experience of the Watcher visions and the transitional experience that occurred in the "Secret Contract" vision involving the Deep Trance and Threshold states of consciousness.

Compared to the bizarre buffet of experiences that were to come, both with respect to identity and locales, the Initiation Narrative of the first week was like an orientation session. It prepared me, the neophyte traveller, for my subsequent journey through the many strange realms that lurked beyond normal consciousness. I had so far only dipped my toes into the shallows of the magical waters of the Tao swirling around me. I had still not shown myself ready to take the plunge into deeper waters, as represented by my visions' inability to move me past the Home realm. The next series of visions showed me that I was ready to move forward and begin my journey into more challenging domains.

The Inception Narrative: The Second Door

A visit by the Anima and leaving home to meet the Teacher,
Followed by the appearance of the second door:
A symbolic portal to multiple realms

16. Vision 6: *The Twins at the Bookshelf*

Vision Matrix

Thematic Narrative: Inception 1 of 4
Session Cluster: 1 of 1
Motif Elements: Vignette, Dialogue, & Judgment

Subject: Identity, Thinking, Myself, Embodied
Content: Visual, Background, Depth, Animated, Navigated
Domain: Human

World Level: Surface World
World Realm: Home
Participation Mode: Embodied Witness
Involvement Level: Passive
Population Level: Populated
Direction of Focus: Left
Consciousness: I-Maginal

"The Twins at the Bookshelf"

My Practice continued into the second week largely unchanged. The one change I did make was to increase the timed length of my meditation to fifty minutes with the ultimate goal of sitting for at least an hour. I continued to employ ambient background music playing off the Internet in my downstairs living room. Later that week I experienced my next vision.

Once again I found myself present in my room as if I were still sitting in meditation within my vision. In the black swirling mist before my seemingly closed eyes an image began to form. As it grew outwards from the center of my visual field its borders took on an irregular oval-like shape, like those thought-bubbles you see in cartoons or the way children would draw clouds in their crayon pictures. Inside the bubble a scene was coming into focus. It seemed like I was getting a look into another dimension as the clouds of mist before my inner eye blew away.

Strangely enough, though I felt myself to be sitting in my room, the scene materializing before me was also in my room, and one that appeared from the perspective of someone sitting in my chair. Right in front of me were all the normal objects present in my room, my carpet, my bookcase with its accompanying clutter, the various pictures and objects hanging on my walls, all visible and well lit. It looked very much like what I had seen on my first two days of meditation when the Watchers had visited me.

My feeling of being present in my room was now three levels deep: (1) myself, sitting in meditation in my room in the external world, (2) imagining myself still in that room in the inner world, and (3) from there, looking out at yet another version of that same room, now in a world one step further removed.

My visions were starting to behave like those nested Russian matryoshka dolls, but with visions of increasing depths nested one inside the other. The Chinese also have a concept of nested box assemblage, one that gives its name to a literary construction in which one narrative is inside another. This is called the "Chinese box structure," which is also known as a "frame narrative."

Fig. 17. The Bookshelf, Another Kind of Nested Box

On this occasion in my imagined room, as in the two earlier cases, it turned out that I was not alone. To the immediate left of my bookshelf stood two figures engaged in conversation, seemingly unaware that they were being observed. They were not the

Watchers from Day 2, however. Rather, they were children, both about ten years old.

The one on the left was a girl with brown hair and pigtails, while on the right was a boy of roughly the same size with short brown hair. They looked very much alike, as if they were brother and sister. They were even dressed similarly. Given that they both appeared to be the same size and age, they might have been fraternal twins. So it seemed to me, at least, at the time. I did not, however, recognize them.

The two children were engaged in a distinct type of repetitive activity. The boy would sometimes lean over and other times kneel down next to the bookcase, at which point he would slide both his gaze and the back of his right hand across a row of books before settling on one to remove. Then, straightening up, he would turn to his left and show the book to the girl, who would examine it and briefly flip through its pages. A discussion about the merits of the book would seem to follow, though it was one I did not hear.

The discussion always ended the same way. The girl would shake her head, sometimes more vigorously than others. She seemed to take pleasure in remaining resolute and resisting his entreaties. The boy, following a halfhearted attempt to defend his choice, would then sigh with resignation and return the book to its spot on the bookshelf. This process repeated itself several times without any resolution until the vision dissolved before my inner eye.

Commentary

Unlike the two Watcher episodes in which the observed participants were aware of my presence but apparently not aware of my cognizance of them, in the case of the "Bookshelf Twins" the two figures were totally immersed in their own activities, which, from the point of view of the unfolding narrative, involved only themselves and no one else. This is why I felt like an intruder eavesdropping on their private affairs. This seemed like another good example of a Sojourn motif, even though it seemed higher resolution than I normally experienced. Was this just a case of cosmically crossed wires?

But the fact was, this episode occurred in my room and revolved about the books sitting in my bookcase. Contrary to the crossed wires analogy, this vision was no accident of transmission.

There was a reason this scenario took place in the same room where I sat in meditation. This vision was connected to me, in spite of the fact that the children seemed to take no notice of my presence. The vignette was being played out for my benefit.

In some ways this vision felt like a continuation of the "Standing Watchers" vision, since both took place in the left side of my room and both involved two individuals. Had the two Watcher men morphed into the two children? Just as the identity of the Watchers had begun as a mystery, so too did that of the two twins.

The little boy might have represented myself as a child, but the presence of the girl was a mystery. I had no sisters nor did I have any girl playmates as a young child, certainly not ones I would have had with me in my room. Of course, this wasn't my childhood room I had seen, but the one in which I was currently meditating. Nor do I have any children or friends with children (although I do have a niece and nephew, both now in their twenties).

Since I received no clues concerning the identity of the children, their identity must not be have been as important as what they symbolized. Three areas of inquiry seem especially important to deciphering this question. First, why were they twins, and in particular, why a boy and a girl? Second, why were they present in my meditation space? And finally, what did the books on the bookshelf represent and why were the twins unable to agree on which one to read?

Yin and Yang

Regarding the first of these questions, the children symbolized to me two complementary aspects of my being, one the Yin or female side and the other the Yang or male side. As I discussed earlier, the Yin side represents the female, dark, hidden, and receptive aspect of phenomena and the Yang the male, light, visible, and active side of things. The girl was on the left side in the vision and the boy, who was on the right, was actively choosing a book and presenting it to the girl who received it, consistent with their representing the Yin and Yang natures. From the standpoint of meditation, the Yin side symbolizes the unconsciousness and the Yang side the consciousness.

In Chinese philosophy Yin and Yang are complementary aspects of a single unity, so that the one is never found without the other, as the *T'ai Chi* diagram shows. That is why the two were presented as twins, two siblings who are as close to being the same person as a boy and a girl could be. The fact that they were children was perhaps an explicit acknowledgement of the very early stage of my meditative practice and my need for much more experience in the ways of its realms.

Anima and Animus

The concepts Yin and Yang can be viewed in Jungian terms as corresponding to the *Anima* and *Animus*. For Jung the Anima represented the forces behind consciousness from which the male's consciousness arose (the Animus). According to Jung, the Anima was not so much the projection of consciousness as it was the projector. It was the

> *"... mirror in which unconsciousness becomes aware of its own face"* (Jung 1953, vol. 14, para. 129);

> *"... the natural archetype that sums up all the statements of the unconscious, of the primitive mind... always the a priori element in his moods, reactions, impulses... It is something that lives of itself, that makes us live; it is a life behind consciousness..."* (Jung 1953, vol. 9, part I, para. 57).

Jung also associated the Anima with the Yin in Chinese philosophy, in particular with the unconscious Animal or Yin Soul *p'o*. Conversely, Yang represented the conscious Yang Soul *hun* or, in its more refined form, the Spirit *shen*. From this perspective, the Anima was the life force of the Yin Soul *p'o* and Animus the consciousness of the Yang Spirit *hun* (or *shen*). For Chinese philosophy, the integrated human Soul would be the harmonious Yin-Yang melding of *p'o-hun*.

Jung had a special term for the distinctive tandem nature of the relationship between paired concepts like Anima and Animus or Soul and Spirit, a relationship he called "syzygy," in which

> *"One is never separated from the Other"* (Jung 1953, vol. 9, part I, para. 194).

I should note that this strange sounding and hard to say word "syzygy" never made it into our popular lexicon, unlike its more successful cousin "synergy." The latter, I believe, has worn out its welcome due to flagrant overuse. The notion of twins, as well as the concepts of Yin and Yang, would have been prime examples of syzygies for Jung, since the existence of one always entailed the existence of the other.

If the girl in the vision represented the Anima or unconscious mind and the boy the Animus or conscious mind, their presence within my meditation space was significant. It was a very clear signal that they were engaged in an activity symbolizing a communication between the unconscious mind (Anima) and my conscious mind (Animus) about my meditative practice. On one level, the books in the vision represented particular elements of what I was thinking at the time about meditation and what it could reveal. The bookshelf would accordingly symbolize the complete set of all my conceptual thoughts and points of view on the subject.

The boy (Animus) was clearly looking for something, much as was I in my Practice. He was counting on the guidance of the girl (Anima) to help him identify if he was on the right track. I didn't get the impression that she was actually giving him much in the way of guidance, however. If anything, she seemed to be constantly putting up roadblocks. His refusal to accept "no" for an answer was either admirable or a juvenile display of stubbornness. Given this persistence in the face of continual rejection, I view his behavior as an example of a Jungian "Child" archetype. This persistence would probably be a quality I would need on my own visionary quest.

Still, the girl could have simply walked away from the bookshelf or even knocked it over like many Zen monks would have done. In that case I would have concluded that my Soul was simply telling me to stop looking for answers and guidance in words and thoughts, much as the *Tao-Te-Ching* had counseled. But instead she reviewed each book offered by the boy. Because she was willing to participate in the review process, one of the messages being conveyed was "keep looking, the answers you seek will come to you, even if they haven't yet."

Of course, the apocryphal saying attributed to Freud that "sometimes a cigar is just a cigar" might apply here. If so, the books would literally represent the works I was currently reading and studying as I took on the challenge of this new discipline. The repeated dissatisfaction of the girl with the reading choices of the boy may have meant that my consciously directed studies were somehow leading me astray or at least not proceeding on the right track.

Given my subconscious' apparent rejection of my existing reading material, I could entertain a couple of different scenarios concerning the deeper meaning of this vision. On the one hand this vision might be a sign that things needed to change and I should look for some new, more fertile areas for my research. I should note that several weeks after this vision I started reading Aurobindo's famous work, *The Life Divine*, and would continue to study it for many months. This vision could have been another example of visionary precognition. On the other hand, maybe the real meaning was that the right book had yet to be written and one of the outcomes of the Practice would be the impetus to attempt such a book myself. Probably all these things are true.

17. Vision 7: *The Illuminated Window*

Vision Matrix

Thematic Narrative: Inception 2 of 4
Session Cluster: 1 of 1
Motif Elements: Illumination, Portal, Window, & Facsimile

Subject: Identity, Myself, Embodied, Imbedded
Content: Visual, Background, Depth, Animated, Navigated
Domain: Human

World Level: Surface World
World Realm: Home
Participation Mode: Embodied Subject
Involvement Level: Passive
Population Level: Solitary
Direction of Focus: Centered
Consciousness: I-Maginal

"The Illuminated Window"

Not too long after the "Bookshelf Twins" vision, I again found myself in the Home realm located within what appeared to be a version of my home. No longer was I in my meditation chair or even in my room. I had left my meditation space entirely and was now traveling down the stairs to the living room and then into the kitchen.

I ultimately ended up standing stationary before my kitchen sink. I was looking straight ahead through the window over the sink towards what would normally have been my back yard. Although I had been moving, at no time did I feel I was in control. I had no sense of my own will or volition. It was as if I were sleepwalking. I felt more like a passenger than a driver.

The orientation and configuration of the kitchen sink and window felt familiar to me, as did the rest of the space surrounding me. In the real world I often found myself at this very spot, staring out the window and rinsing off dishes before putting them in the dishwasher. In this vision there were no dishes, and apparently I was just standing there, doing nothing. No one else was present. There were no sounds. Nor did I experience any thoughts or feelings beyond the feeling of simple familiarity.

Fig. 18. The Real Kitchen Window

But although I initially recognized the kitchen layout as that of my kitchen and felt at home there, by the end of the vision it was no longer my kitchen. Its features had morphed into something different, but without my having noticed or responded to the changes as they were happening around me.

Part of my complacency might have been due to the fact that many elements of the kitchen maintained their initial positions throughout the vision. The sink remained in the same place, as did the adjacent counter tops. The window kept its same dimensions and was still above the sink. From the standpoint of its layout, the room was still recognizable as my kitchen.

Although the relative configurations of all these components remained constant, by the end of my vision almost everything else had changed. The sink, which on the inside had been round on one half and square on the other, was now rectangular in shape, with a rough hewed finish like you might see on a utility sink. Instead of the single handle, pull-down, stainless steel kitchen faucet, there now sat an old-fashioned faucet with a squarish spout and cross handles, one on each side. The tile work surrounding the sink had also disappeared, to be replaced by an unfinished stone surface.

Where before had been a transparent sliding two-piece square bay window, recessed above the sink looking into the backyard, there was now one window set flush with the wall above the sink, made out of a thick solid pane of semi-translucent material. The trees in the yard were no longer visible. Only bright white light showed through the window.

My kitchen had regressed in time to an era when design was purely utilitarian in nature and materials were crude and rough. The window especially had devolved to the point where it had lost most of its transparency and let only diffuse light shine into the room. What was happening on the other side of the window remained unknown.

Part of me later wondered whether the outside world had disappeared. Had some force within the light dissolved everything except the room where I was standing? Was the metamorphosis of the room a sign that it too was in the process of dissolution? Would I have been next if I hadn't soon returned to Threshold consciousness?

Looking out through this window I experienced a strong force pulling me towards the increasingly bright light, as if the window were an open gateway beckoning me into another dimension. For reasons internal to the logic of the vision, I experienced no reaction to this phenomenon or any awareness of the strange metamorphosis that was occurring in the kitchen. Everything seemed completely natural to me. It was only after I returned to normal consciousness that I was able to reflect on the events that had transpired in this vision.

Commentary

This vision represented a situation that shared more in common with normal experience than with the other visions I had previously seen, at least during the first part of the vision. Leaving my room and walking down the stairs to go into the kitchen is something I have done many thousands of times, as was standing before the sink to look out the kitchen window onto my back deck. This was the first time in a vision that I stood up and moved. It was also the first time I left one room for another.

However, though I initially ended up in a version of my own kitchen, that element of normalcy didn't last. The objects in the kitchen changed their shape, and as a result, what had been the kitchen window took on a new symbolic significance. It became an illuminated portal looking out onto an unknown realm.

The Attention Test

As I wrote this section I was reminded of the famous "The New SKODA Fabia Attention Test" video (a car commercial) that I recently saw on the Internet. On this video the viewer is shown a street scene with a car at its center. Over the course of about 65 seconds multiple elements within the scene change while the viewer is distracted by dark flashes every four seconds or so. By the end of the video a completely different street scene is present, though most watchers would not notice everything had changed. This seemed similar to what I experienced in my vision of the kitchen, since I demonstrated no reaction to the changes occurring around me.

In the before and after images in the car video, the general shapes, arrangement and types of objects in the scene stayed the same. There were two automobiles, one blue and one black, and a two-wheeled vehicle to the left. There were four buildings with storefronts and centered windows above them facing a static street. But beyond these general features, pretty much everything else about the scene was different. This video is an example of what is called "change blindness."

At the end of this video a gorilla is shown mysteriously seated on the roof of the white building on the left. This serves as homage to the famous "Selective Attention Test" video of Chabris and Simons. In their video a person in a gorilla suit walked through two teams of players, one wearing white and the other black, who passed basketballs to members of their team. Most viewers did not see the gorilla because they were focused on the task of counting the number of times the players wearing white shirts passed the ball.

Selective attention scenarios like these take advantage of several tendencies associated with the human mind in its everyday operation. First, the mind has a type of tunnel vision that ignores things happening on the periphery of its focused attention. Second, the mind has a built-in bias towards ignoring events outside its normal situational expectations. Third, other things being equal, the mind will assume that the general features of the background environment will remain constant.

These factors are why the narratives portrayed in these videos maintained their coherence in spite of the presence of anomalous data. But I do not believe these kinds of factors explain my behavior in the situation where my kitchen morphed around me.

It is true that within the "Illuminated Window" vision my mind did successfully ignore the presence of the rapidly spreading cognitive dissonance. But this did not mean that I was not fully aware of the narrative unfolding before me, or more importantly, that this awareness was not a necessary part of the vision's content.

Within the vision I did initially see the trees through the window and later just diffuse white light. I did see the modern sink from my kitchen and then its much more primitive version. When the vision was over, I was able to recall the anomalous elements of the experience. This was unlike the viewers of the selective attention videos who had no memory of the changes to the street scene or the presence of the gorilla.

Another Kind of Test

These observations reveal something important. This vision was another example of the kinds of tests the Soul had presented me with in earlier visions, where it assessed my reactions before allowing me to move forward. In this case the test was whether I would be able to embrace the process of metamorphosis so prevalent in visionary experiences. My recognition and acceptance of this process was essential to my ability to successfully progress along the visionary path. It signified my acknowledgement that different rules and logics applied within the Soul's realms. If I were to travel in its realms, I needed to successfully navigate the plasticity and ambiguities existing in these new realities.

Through the Looking Glass

The "Illuminated Window" vision marked a transition point in the early part of my journey along the mystical path of the Tao. It took place within the Home realm, but differed in significant ways from the preceding visions of this realm.

Unlike the three earlier visions within my imagined home, this was the first in which I was an observer of the content of the vision and an actual subject moving within the vision. In the other visions I was simply an unobserved observer, at least from the standpoint of the participants of the visions. It is true that a version of myself had been under observation in the two Watcher visions. But in these instances my awareness of their presence had gone undetected. The possibility of my ever becoming aware of them seemed inconsistent with the internal logic of the narrative. To them I was simply the object of their attention. I was not someone for them to engage in conversation or for whom they would have to modify their behavior.

Secondly, this was the first time within a vision that I left the space of my meditation room, even if it was just to go downstairs to the kitchen. That was the beginning of increasing progress along the visionary path, however small the virtual distance initially travelled. The fact that I felt a force pulling me towards the kitchen window probably indicated that I was getting close to the moment when I would finally leave the safe confines of my visionary home in order to explore new and more challenging vistas within the Practice. Maybe this was the same force that pulled me out of my chair in the first place and brought me down to the kitchen window.

Finally, while the depiction of the room in the earlier visions was admittedly not a fine-grained or entirely accurate representation of the real thing, it was accurate enough to be recognized both in the vision and afterwards as a faithful facsimile of my meditation space. In addition, and perhaps more significantly, it was a stable and solidly appearing representation. It was not the primary subject of the vision but instead the backdrop against which the vision played out. In the "Illuminated Window" vision the background had now become the foreground, no longer just a virtual space but an actual participant and subject of the vision.

On the other hand, I, as the observer within the vision, had now become a static object in the scene, unmoving and unmoved. I did nothing but stand there as the kitchen morphed into something both itself and not itself, a kitchen but not my kitchen, at the same time as the world outside the window dissolved into a featureless and increasingly bright haze.

In some ways the kitchen was no longer a kitchen but the expression of the Platonic form of a kitchen, constantly changing in appearance while maintaining the integrity of its essential nature. Perhaps all the different kitchen versions stored in the Platonic archive were being purposefully cycled through the vision's narrative in order to convey a Buddhist-like truth about the impermanence of appearances.

In the new rules of the visionary realm the presence of objects within a scene assumed new meaning and significance. Sometimes they were features of the background, mere props for the visionary experience. Other times they took on a life of their own, becoming the primary actors within the scene, symbolizing more than just an inanimate hollow shell. In these kinds of cases there were no more objects, no things that remained stable and unmoving until acted upon by outside forces.

Within the vision, internal forces were the drivers of change. In general, things no longer existed; they were now processes, *a la* Whitehead, evolving and transforming as necessary to reflect the contingencies of the visionary narrative. The only thing that reliably existed now was the visionary narrative. The only rules that mattered were the ones the narrative supplied. As Dorothy said, "Toto, I've a feeling we're not in Kansas anymore." Truer words were never spoken.

18. Vision 8: The *Spirit Dancers*

Vision Matrix

Thematic Narrative: Inception 3 of 4
Session Cluster: 1 of 1
Motif Elements: Dialogue, Teacher, Multiplicity, Rainbow, & Tree

Subject: Identity, Thinking, Myself, Embodied, Imbedded
Content: Visual, Background, Depth, Animated, Navigated
Domain: Human, Symbolic

World Level: Surface World
World Realm: Home
Participation Mode: Embodied Subject
Involvement Level: Passive
Population Level: Populated
Direction of Focus: Left
Consciousness: I-Maginal

"The Spirit Dancers"

In my next vision, I was still within the familiar surroundings of the Home realm, though I was, as Dorothy said, no longer in Kansas. It was a week or so later. The forward momentum that had begun in the "Illuminated Window" vision had apparently persisted and provided me with enough acceleration to finally escape the confining gravity of my house, albeit now to another place where I spent significant time almost every day.

That place was the local health club, my home away from home. I probably spent as much time there as I did at home sitting in meditation. While I was there, I would also typically achieve a different form of altered consciousness, one brought on by intense exercise. Not surprisingly, what was to transpire in my vision was not the usual health club experience. It was also very different from the highly circumscribed type of visions I had so far experienced.

This was to be the first stop on my journey down what was to become my own Yellow Brick Road.

As my vision came into focus, I found myself in the parking lot of one of those local strip malls that are so ubiquitous in modern America. I don't remember much about the appearance of the buildings in the mall, only that the storefronts all had large areas of semi-transparent glass windows facing the lot. I recall stepping out of my car and looking down at the black pavement, seeing the white stripes of the parking spaces, almost as if this was needed to ground me within the scene.

Apparently, having graduated from simply sitting or standing around immobile in my house, now I had been driving about in cars. Strangely enough, my real health club at the time was not located in a two-story strip mall, but in a multi-level office building, though the scene in this vision looked very much like a place I would visit a year later while my normal club was being relocated.

Had this been another instance of the psychic foreshadowing I had experienced in the past? I don't think this was the case. More likely this strip mall, along with the one in the real world I was later to visit, was an amalgamation of all the health club locations I had been to in the past, a sad expression of the Platonic form of the American shopping center.

I walked across the parking lot and pulled open the glass-paneled door, entering the facility. To the left, there was a counter, behind which stood the customary welcoming attendant, a cheerful young woman in a colored polo shirt. We talked briefly, and she directed me down the corridor to my right, into the building.

I remember that I was not dressed in workout gear, nor did I have the expected gym bag with me. Instead I was dressed in jeans and a casual collared shirt. I should note that I never dress this way in real life. Why was I dressed in Silicon Valley casual? On whom was I trying to make a good impression? Clearly this wasn't a job interview, but perhaps my Soul knew it to be some other kind of test and dressed me accordingly. I was there to check out the facility and, in particular, a group class currently in session. This class was the reason I was considering joining the club.

Proceeding into the hallway I turned and opened a door to my right, stepping into a large room. The room initially appeared configured like the standard yoga studio, with wood floors and mirrors on the walls. The ceiling looked higher than normal, with hanging lights providing a soft illumination that merged with gently pulsing waves of reflected colored light.

I heard music coming from inside, sounding very much like the ambient music I played in the background while I meditated. The music had no melody or structure to it, yet nonetheless was very hypnotic. It had an ethereal quality to it, much more so than the standard ambient fare I was usually listening to. I wondered whether I had mistakenly stumbled into a yoga or meditation class.

As I entered the room I became aware of the presence of people to my left and turned towards them. What I saw quickly dissuaded me that this was a typical health club class. I saw three rows of people, with six per row. They were lined up on the planks of a raised wooden platform, with each row a couple of feet above the next. The stage looked like the choir riser platforms you might see in a church. It was not what you would expect to find in a health club's yoga studio.

The people were not attired like normal health club members either. Like in a church choir, everyone was wearing long white robes over their street clothes. Their robes took on subtle rainbow-like hues as the lights in the room washed over them. Their hands and arms were swaying above their head, with their whole bodies undulating to the rhythms of the music. Small groups of them moved in unison with others. They coordinated their movements with each other and the beat of the music. I found this very odd, especially since there was no beat. "How could they be dancing to ambient music?" I asked myself. But they were dancing and with a high degree of precision.

I also noticed how flexible and loose-jointed the dancers appeared. They moved as if they lacked normal human bone structure. Must have been all that yoga, I supposed. They looked very much like aquatic plants swaying in the moving water of a stream. They also reminded me of those inflated dancing tube people you often see outside carwashes. They were not young people, but middle-aged and older adults, made up of approximately equal numbers of men and women. Given their ability to move in response to the purely ambient music and their flowing white robes, I later named them the "Spirit Dancers."

Proceeding towards this group, I was approached on my left in front of the riser platform by a woman I took to be the leader of the class (the Teacher). She was a little younger than the participants of the group, in her upper thirties, but wearing street clothes very similar to what I was wearing. She was about my height, with long straight brown hair parted in the middle. She actually looked like an adult version of the little girl I had seen in in the "Bookshelf Twins" vision. She immediately engaged me in conversation, though I don't remember specifically what she said at first.

The Teacher quickly directed my attention to the left end of the room in front of the risers, where I saw a table. Resting on this table was a metallic, tree-shaped object about three feet tall with spherical colored mirrors of various hues hanging from flexible arms like leaves on branches. As these mirrors vibrated and bounced off each other, tracing different patterns in the air, they radiated a complex pattern of light with constantly shifting hues. There appeared to be three main branches on the object, with six orbs branching off each one. Each orb had its own color, with no colors being repeated. I'll refer to this object as the "Mirror Tree."

The resulting patterns of light reminded me a little of the mirrored disco balls that started appearing during the psychedelic period of the late 1960s. Was this vision a '60s era flashback, I wondered? The dancers *were* moving a lot like people did during that period when they were under the influence of psychedelic mood enhancers.

I was puzzled about where the music was coming from, since there were no speakers or any other potential sources in the room. Nor was the music audible outside the room. I asked the Teacher where the source of the music was. Instead of answering me, she indicated via gestures that she would rather show me instead.

The Teacher turned back towards the Spirit Dancers and the Mirror Tree and raised her arms with her palms up, as if trying to get everyone's attention. She held this pose for a few seconds and then lowered her arms with her palms down. The dancers all stopped as one. But so did the music and the flashing lights, at seemingly the same moment as the dancers.

Continuing her demonstration, she then gestured for them to begin moving again. As soon as she did, the music and the lights came back on and the dancers started moving again. I wasn't sure about the exact sequence. The Teacher then turned back towards me, raising her eyebrows in my direction. Her face and demeanor seemed to ask, "Do you understand now?" Despite my best efforts I did not.

The Teacher smiled as she observed my expressions of puzzlement and gently shook her head. Had she somehow heard my thoughts? She said that the kinds of energetic transformations I was witnessing were very subtle and not easily understood. Was she talking about the Spirit Dancers? I was still puzzled.

The Teacher, sensing my continued confusion, explained why I was having this particular experience. My presence here was not by accident. She told me that I had previously been invited and had agreed to come. She said that all individuals who visited her in this place were shown a venue specifically tailored to their backgrounds and their ability to understand her message.

She added that only the individuals who were successfully able to visit this place would be candidates for further training. This was the reason I was here today, she said. She asked if I was prepared to pledge myself to further study on this path. Was she asking me if I wished to join the chorus and become a SpiritDancer? I don't recall what my answer was. Maybe I had already given my answer by the fact of my presence. As I turned to leave the room, the vision faded away.

Commentary

This vision was noteworthy for many reasons, including the many firsts it included. It was the first time I had traveled outside my home, freely moving through several different locations. It was the first time I perceived sound, beyond the conversational voices that I had been hearing as thoughts. It was the first time that subjects in the vision interacted with me and me them.

But even though I was an embodied subject within the vision, my main purpose there was to act as an observer to whatever my Soul had intended to reveal. It was as if I were a student being lectured to by the Teacher character. Fundamentally my role was still passive. I would have to pass through several more series of visions and different realms before I ceased being a passive spectator and became a more active participant in the narratives unfolding around me.

The other significant aspect of this vision was the way the internal narrative had become so complex that it folded back upon itself like a lucid dream and revealed to me that I was present within a vision. The Teacher, a character within the vision, called my attention to this fact, much as the Trickster had done so long ago. On the basis of Jung's work and given the Teacher's revelations, I believe the Teacher was a representation of the Anima of the Soul. The Anima used the symbolism of this vision in conjunction with the Teacher's dialogue to communicate with me, the Animus persona.

The fact that other characters were present besides the Teacher was also important to this vision's symbolism. The rows of white robed dancers were a prominent feature of the vision. They were arrayed on the raised platform like some wayward church choir that had suddenly been dropped into this strange venue. Something about their white robes and the rising steps on which they stood must have been important for understanding the meaning of this vision.

Using the concepts of Yin and Yang that I employed in earlier chapters, I suggest as a preliminary interpretation that the movements of the white robed dancers, the Spirit Dancers, portrayed the process through which the coordination of different frequencies of Yang Spirit energy resulted in the creation of a new type of experience. Each row of dancers represented a particular wavelength of sound and color, with each step on the platform depicting a higher frequency. Each dancer on a given step could likewise symbolize a musical note or color.

The fact that the dancers were conducted and trained by the Teacher, who represented the figure of the Jungian Anima, indicated something about the way the unconscious forces of the Soul shaped the perception of higher-order experiences by the conscious Animus, represented by the presence of my persona within the vision. But I still have not accounted for the role played by the Mirror Tree in this vision.

Seeing Sounds

Whatever the role of the Mirror Tree, it must be connected with the spectrum of colors reflected by its mirrors. The apparent causal relationship between the colors and musical sounds in this vision suggested an equivalency of color and sound, one that in fact has a basis in reality. Both color and sound have their origins in the patterned frequency modulations of electro-magnetic (EM) waves, though at very different ends of the EM spectrum.

For example, the frequency for the pitch A4 is 440 Hz (waves per second), while the frequency for the color red is 430 trillion Hz.

By conceptually stepping up frequencies across many orders of magnitude in a manner that preserved octaves, lower frequency sound waves could be mapped to their corresponding level on the much higher frequency visible scale. For example, the pitch A4 at an ultrahigh octave is in the orange color range.

Given the fact we perceive both colors and musical notes as discrete spectral tones, it is not surprising that the question of possible correlations between their frequencies went all the way back to the ancient Greeks. There have been numerous proposed mappings between the seven colors and the seven notes of the scale, including some by such luminaries as Isaac Newton and Goethe.

In the 18th century the first "color organs" began to be constructed, using a piano keyboard to produce both light and sound. Those of us who lived through the psychedelic 1960's probably remember the prolific presence of light organs in the dance halls, which bathed the participants in waves of colored light, much like in my vision. This vision may have partly come out of memories from that era.

Additional interest in this correspondence also came from the study of a rare neurological condition in which stimulation of one sensory pathway elicited experiences within another sensory pathway. This condition is known as "synesthesia." The particular form of synesthesia in which sounds are associated with colors is known as "chromesthesia" and is the most common variant of this condition.

Many well-known musicians (Sibelius, Rimsky-Korsakov, Liszt), artists (Van Gogh, Whistler, Kandinsky), and writers (Baudelaire, Rimbaud, Nabokov) have been identified as synesthetes. Some of these artists explicitly attributed their creative breakthroughs to these synesthetic experiences.

The Mystery of the Mirror Tree

There is more to this vision than just its illustration of the vibrational correspondence between colors and sounds. The vision presented me with an explicit mystery concerning the origin of the music and the role of the Mirror Tree. And it made this mystery a major component of its narrative. This is significant, for it demonstrated the strength of my commitment to the reality of the situation. Where else could I have tried to solve this mystery except right there where I believed it was happening? I was clearly fully immersed in the experience.

It is true that in previous visions I also engaged in various degrees of reflection. But that was the product either of my disembodied awareness watching the scene from an external point of view, or my embodied visionary self still believing itself engaged in the act of meditation. While the Teacher knew I was still inside a vision, my visionary character did not. In this vision I tried to understand what I was experiencing as a participant within the vision, drawing upon cognitive faculties usually associated with a degree of consciousness at least as robust as that of the Threshold level.

There is another aspect to this vision that demonstrated my continued connection to Threshold consciousness. I heard the music in a very different way from how I experienced the conversation with the Teacher. As was the case in almost all my visions, the conversation was telepathic in nature, appearing as spoken words within my thoughts, not at all how I normally perceived spoken sound. The music, however, did have the quality of sound I associated with normal sensory perception.

Because some connection to Threshold consciousness had apparently persisted in this vision, this suggests a different explanation for the source of the music. The music I heard in the vision was not entirely generated within the vision. Rather, it was a modulated and distorted form of the music I was still hearing in my room while sitting in meditation. Elements of the music from the external world had been allowed by my Soul to leak into this inner realm to be used as a key element of its narrative.

The existence of this open channel provides a solution to the mystery of the role of the Mirror Tree. Since the music was being generated on a plane external to the visionary realm, it needed a portal to enter the vision's arena. The Mirror Tree represented that portal. The sound waves coming into the Mirror Tree resulted in patterns of movement through its mirrored spheres, which were then reflected as colored light across the space of the room. The Mirror Tree transmutes waves of sound into those of color, much like the inner ear's structure transmutes waves of sound into mechanical energy. From the point of view of the narrative, only light entered the vision, not sound.

These waves of light are therefore a significant component of the vision's narrative. The Spirit Dancers reacted to these colored lights by responding to the light energies pulsing against them. The patterns of movement that resulted in turn created the different vibrational frequencies in the air perceived by me as sound. They were dancing to the waves of light, not to the sound. The sound was the aftereffect. The rhythmic movement of the Spirit Dancers reminds me of the behavior of hair cells in the inner ear, which stimulate auditory nerves as the vibrations in the surrounding fluid sweep over them.

As the Anima, the Teacher played the role of the conjuring magician, creating and sustaining the illusion projected within the vision even as she was a participating character within it. Her gestures, much like those of a symphonic conductor, integrated the modulated energies flowing off the Mirror Tree with the movements of the Spirit Dancers. At the same time, she kept the channel to Threshold consciousness open.

The Teacher did not stop the music by freezing the movements of the Spirit Dancers; she did so by closing the portal to the Mirror Tree. In this respect she was acting in the role of gatekeeper. When the Mirror Tree stopped moving, the dancers stopped moving, and so did the music.

From the perspective of the characters in the vision, forces outside their normal realm drove the movements of the tree and dancers, since the Mirror Tree vibrated to energies from a hidden realm (Threshold consciousness). In this interior domain the music that we typically take for granted was experienced as something mysterious, emerging from some unknown realm. This was a demonstration of the strange kind of inversion that occurred within the visionary universe, where the conscious became the unconscious and the unconscious the conscious.

Emergence and Unified Consciousness

This vision gave me a look into the unconscious processes of harmonious creation, as told through the example of ambient music. It suggested that the experiences of the outside world are the direct result of the integrating activities of hidden forces. At the same time it illustrated one way emergent experiences of the kind described by Wilber could be generated.

Key to this process was the guided interplay (conducted by the Anima) of separate elements (the Spirit Dancers) whose coordinated movements created higher order patterns of vibrating energy. From these overlapping patterns entirely new forms of musical experience emerged that were witnessed in consciousness (by the Animus).

This process illustrates the two-fold nature of the holarchical type of emergence discussed by Wilber. It shows both the synthesis of higher order experiences (music) from a collection of lower order ones (light pulses perceived by the Spirit Dancers), as well as the transitional stages between one form of consciousness and the next (from the Animus to the Anima to the Animus). A key characteristic of the process of emergence is the transition from multiple discrete phenomena at one level to a unified wavelike experience at a higher level, or, in more concrete terms, the transformation of digital input into analog output.

This vision might also be saying something about the process of unified consciousness generation in the brain. Neuroscience believes that integrated consciousness emerges from the activation and deactivation of networks of neurons in our brains. This process might be a real world example of the synthesis of higher order experiences depicted in this vision.

The movements of the Spirit Dancers could symbolize the changing patterns of energized neurons as they turned off and on. The resulting energy vibrations would create wavelike patterns in the surrounding air that would be experienced as unified consciousness (the ambient music).

Two scientists, Susan Pockett and Johnjoe McFadden, have formulated a theory of consciousness remarkably similar to this, called "*cemi*," or the "Conscious Electromagnetic Field Theory" (Pocket 2000). The theory holds that it is not the on/off patterns of neurons that generate consciousness, but rather specific fluctuations in the surrounding electromagnetic (EM) field that are induced by the EM activities of these neurons, much as the surrounding air in the vision was perturbed by the movements of the Spirit Dancers, leading to the experience of music.

Keeping the Thread

The carefully coordinated movements of the Spirit Dancers were clearly an integral part of this vision. In fact, the type of seamless integration displayed by the Spirit Dancers had an additional meaning beyond the ones already discussed, symbolically representing skills I needed to develop for my Practice to be similarly coherent. In this interpretation each dancer represented a vision, with the three step levels depicting the Lower, Surface, and Upper Worlds. The harmonious music created by their integrated movements symbolized the coherent evolution of my visionary journey as I moved between realms and Worlds, much as a musician moves through a score.

One aspect of this coherence pertains to my movement between different states of consciousness. This involves the ability to maintain some amount of situational awareness as I drift from the Threshold consciousness of meditative sitting into the visionary realms of I-Maginal consciousness, and then back again. I experienced an example of the former in the "Bookshelf Twins" vision. Based on my own experience, I realize that developing this kind of intra-sessional capacity is very challenging. This is a skill carefully cultivated by shamanic practitioners in their journeys from the Middle to the Upper or Lower Worlds.

But equally important to the refinement of the Practice is a different kind of seamless integration, one in which the trajectories through different visions will be inter-visionally and inter-sessionally seamless, smoothly integrating elements and themes from earlier visions and sessions into later ones.

The most significant example of this type of integration was this vision's assertion that it was a continuation of an on-going narrative theme begun in earlier visions. The thread of this theme could be seen as unfolding in the following way.

Initially, the Watchers had reviewed my meditative practice and discussed ways to help me progress. An agreement was subsequently reached between myself and another party, perhaps the Teacher. According to this last vision, that agreement was my acceptance of the Teacher's invitation to visit her and acknowledge her role as my helping spirit. Following this acknowledgement I travelled down a symbolic tunnel and experienced a vision of my third eye opening. At that point I was able to begin the next stage of my visionary odyssey, leaving behind my original meditation space. I then began the first stages of my travel further out into the visionary realms, making one of my stops at this early but pivotal junction in my journey, where I would for the first time explicitly meet the Teacher.

The Helping Spirit

One of the questions at this point concerns the identity of the woman Teacher, whom I have been interpreting from the standpoint of the Anima. The Jungian tradition views the Teacher as a representation of the unconscious Soul, whose primary mode of communication with the conscious mind was the language of symbolic imagery rather than words. The Teacher was very sparse with her words.

This reticence can be seen in a couple of ways. For example, when I asked about the role of the Mirror Tree, instead of explaining she provided me with a demonstration. When I incorrectly interpreted the meaning of her demonstration, she merely smiled and made oblique references to subtle energies and further training, which I initially took as an invitation to join the Spirit Dancers. At no point did she offer any explicit account of the meaning of what I was experiencing, even when asked to do so.

The Shamanic tradition supplies an alternative interpretation for the Teacher. Shamanic teachings and practices have appeared in many cultures across the world, including ancient China. In fact, many scholars believe Taoist philosophy evolved from an earlier form of shamanic religion (Wong 1997). Shamanism believes in the independent existence of spirit-like entities associated both with animate and inanimate objects. These spirits are said to visit us in our dreams and visions.

Shamanic tradition acknowledges the importance of helping spirits, who appear within seekers' visions to provide assistance. In these visions practitioners can ask them for guidance and advice. These helpers are not viewed as elements of the practitioner's unconscious or Soul, but as independent spirits active within different World levels. Though they often take the form of animal spirits rather than humans, they are said to be able to talk to you in your vision. But this would only happen if you explicitly engage them in communication and ask direct questions. Of course, even when they give you answers, these often would be in the form of riddles.

Irrespective of which tradition is most appropriate for understanding the role of the Teacher, answers weren't going to come easily in the visionary realm. Was the Teacher a denizen of my own unconscious realm or a separately existing spirit? She implied that the latter was the case within the vision, saying that others had visited her before in visionary settings specifically tailored for them. But was this just another riddle concealing a deeper truth? Was she too an agent of the Trickster?

This question is important because its answer will tell us a great deal about the forces of the Soul active within our unconscious. These forces conceivably have a significant role in the generation of our conscious thoughts and behaviors. If the Teacher appearing in my consciousness truly is a helping spirit visiting me to render assistance, the implication is that practitioners engaged in other forms of spiritual journeying might also experience her presence as well, although in a form more appropriate to them.

19. Vision 9: *The Gateway Portals*

Vision Matrix

Thematic Narrative: Inception 4 of 4
Session Cluster: 1 of 1
Motif Elements: Exit, Hub, Portal, Window, & Tree

Subject: Identity, Thinking, Myself
Content: Visual, Animated
Domain: Human, Symbolic

World Level: Surface World
World Realm: Formal
Participation Mode: Disembodied Witness
Involvement Level: Passive
Population Level: Empty
Direction of Focus: Right
Consciousness: I-Maginal

"The Gateway Portals"

The last vision in this first book is a very simple one. It is one of the most familiar images we see in our interactions with the digital world. Within the visionary realm, of course, this image simultaneously takes on a form both instantly recognizable and indecipherably strange. Like an earlier vision, it too presents itself as a window into another possible realm.

This vision occurred within a few days of the "Spirit Dancers" vision. It started out as an empty expanse of whiteness floating before my disembodied gaze. This whiteness was not diffuse or permeable, however. It was a solid surface of white, like you might see on the blank page of a book.

Soon, however, an image began to come into focus. A column of multiple lines of printed symbols appeared on the white background. Each cluster was separated from the others by intervening areas of white space. There appeared to be about eight such clusters on the page floating before me. The top line of each cluster was larger than the other lines and was purple in color. The other lines were black. Schematically, the page was organized as a tree-like structure with textual branches (the purple lines) and leaves (the black lines).

Was I looking at a page in a book? As my gaze began to travel down from the top of the image towards its lower edge, however, the first lines of each cluster in turn became larger and brighter. It wasn't a book. I realized it was a page on a computer screen. I still wasn't able to read what I took to be the lines of text, but at this point I finally recognized what I was seeing. It was a floating browser window containing what looked like a page from a Google search. I wondered whether the top line of each cluster was the link to some location in the psychic web.

The image became larger and more resolved as my gaze continued to zoom into the page. I hoped that soon I would be able to read what the lines of text were saying. Maybe my visions were ready to provide me with some real clues to help me navigate my journey.

But as the individual characters finally became legible, I realized with a start that I was staring at what appeared to be gibberish. The lines were organized in what looked like sequences of words of various lengths, but the words were themselves completely illegible. This was not because the words were composed of nonsensical sequences of letters. Rather, the font was completely cryptic, so that the words were nothing more than different length strings of indecipherable symbols.

I tried to focus on the symbols to determine if I was able to recognize any of them. I remember thinking that some characters looked familiar, like they had been drawn from a hybrid mixture of elements from Egyptian hieroglyphics and the Hebrew, Greek, and Chinese alphabets, for example. But at other times these characters looked more fantastical, like examples of what I had seen portrayed by so-called paranormal investigators as facsimiles of "angelic" or "alien" scripts.

I wondered if I was being presented with some variant of a substitution code, in which strange symbols took the place of the normal letters of the alphabet in order to hide the real meaning of the text. I'm actually pretty good at cracking these kinds of cyphers, but not within the few seconds allowed me in this vision. Certainly unconscious forces could have spontaneously translated these symbols for me, but clearly they had some other agenda in mind.

While continuing to focus my attention on the individual characters in an attempt to recognize them, something strange began to happen. Individual pixels started to emerge from the characters and float off towards the upper right corner of my field of view, as if the characters were beginning to boil. It was like the characters were starting to disintegrate before my very eyes. The pixels themselves were multi-colored and swirling around each other. They reminded me of the kinds of patterns swarms of insects might make on a warm summer evening around a street lamp.

As the pixels continued to evaporate off the characters, I realized that the characters were not so much disintegrating as they were morphing into different shapes. At some point in this process the characters suddenly became recognizable and legible words began to form. I quickly turned my focus back onto the lines of text in an attempt to read what was there. Either I was not quick enough or what I had seen was erased from my memory, for I have no memory of what, if anything, I was able to read there. The letters became fainter and fainter as their pixels continued to fly away. This dissolution accelerated in speed with each attempt by me to look closer and resolve the characters.

The continuing flight of pixels from the characters was soon joined by the pixels from the white background. As the white pixels boiled off, areas of dark vibrating pixels began to appear in their place, like black blemishes growing on a field of white. The white background continued to fade away, growing darker and darker as more of its pixels left.

Soon all that remained was the diffuse shimmering irregular black field that I knew so well. I realized then that I was sitting in meditation within Threshold consciousness. I had successfully maintained my awareness through the interstitial border region that connected I-Maginal with Threshold consciousness. I had witnessed one form of the process by which a visionary state lost its resolution and faded back into normal meditation consciousness.

Commentary

The appearance of the Google search page was significant because in its normal use it serves as our portal to the universe of the public Internet (the dark web is a whole different story). The appearance of this type of portal in my vision suggests the existence of a similar portal to my unconscious, providing me potential access to the many inner realms in the Soul's hidden Worlds.

If this vision represented a passageway, it was different from the way these normally appeared in visions, even ignoring the abstract way it was displayed. It wasn't a doorway, or a corridor, or a path to a particular location. Rather, it was a gateway to a number of potential destinations, more like a train station or an airport terminal. This type of portal is an example of the Hub motif.

The difficulty with this vision's efficacy as a terminal, of course, was that all the signs for describing the alternative destinations were written in a foreign language. It was like I was trapped in a foreign airport where all the signs were displayed in an inaccessible script and no translators were available.

The other odd feature of this vision is subtler and concerns the color of the top line of text in each cluster. In the Google results window the first line normally is the title of the web page matched by the search query, and is also a link to that page. When the results page first appears, all the titles are in blue. These titles only become purple after they are clicked and their links are used to bring up the associated web page. The fact that all the titles were purple in my vision meant that all the destinations represented on the page had already been visited.

Since the destination titles in the vision were indecipherable and yet nevertheless had been visited, I came to two conclusions. First, the interface I saw was not one I was able to use at that time. It might have been a test to see if I had the mental focus to use it, something I clearly didn't. Perhaps it was a preview of a facility that would be available to me sometime in the future for navigating the visionary realms, but only after I had received sufficient experience to do so. Or maybe it was a glimpse of an area in my subconscious that I was never supposed to see. If so, it was a place I had stumbled upon by accident in my meditation. This would explain why it so quickly dissolved when I tried to focus on it.

The other message I found in the vision concerned the fact that someone else had already been using this interface to travel to the locations listed on the symbolic Google page. I was clearly intended to ponder who that someone else might be. I assume that this someone else must be a personified representation of some aspect of the Soul, such as the Teacher or that mysterious "I" figure from the "Secret Contract" vision.

But there is still more to this particular interpretation. This listing of destinations was presented as a Google result page, rather than as a simple menu on a web home page. Because this vision utilized a Google result page, the implication was that someone first had to enter a query in the home page's search box before this result page could appear.

What might that query have been? Perhaps it was some question I had been pondering consciously or even subconsciously. If so, what I saw in the vision would be a figurative representation of the response of the Soul to that question.

Besides these unanswered questions that followed from the vision, there were also clear meanings that could be found in it. These related back to previous visions. As was the case in the "Illuminated Window" vision, this vision involved a window opening up into a white expanse, which could also be viewed as a portal into another realm. But unlike the "Illuminated Window," in which the nature of the other realm was left obscure and undefined, this vision explicitly revealed a series of potential destinations that could be accessed. If my recall is correct, the page in the vision showed eight discrete locations.

These destinations, which ran from top to bottom, might also have been ranked in terms of some significance or priority, as they would have been on a real Google results page. So, while this vision did not reveal anything about the nature of these destinations, it did tell me that there were at least eight discrete locations I could visit, ones that had been prioritized in some kind of order.

Transitions

This vision also had elements related to my interpretation of the "Spirit Dancers" vision. One of the ways I viewed that vision was as a symbolic representation showing the process of transformation of energies from the internal unconscious mind into their representation in external consciousness. The "Gateway Portals" vision might represent a similar process.

This vision showed the way in which the unconscious mind's normally hidden processing of a query from the conscious mind could be expressed in familiar symbolism. In both these visions, even though the symbols were familiar ones, their meaning was not completely clear.

Another key aspect of the "Spirit Dancers" vision was the concept of seamless integration expressed within that vision. I had previously interpreted that concept in terms of the smoothness of the transition both between visions and visionary states of consciousness. I have already described several examples of that first type of transition.

This is the first instance of the second type. The "Gateway Portals" vision is the first time when I was able to maintain conscious awareness during the transition from I-Maginal back into Threshold consciousness. In all my previous visionary experiences, the departure from I-Maginal consciousness had been an abrupt one.

This is not just the first case of a seamless transition from one state of consciousness to another, however. There is another aspect to this experience. The fact that this vision made this transition so overt and recognizable by using a pixelization process strongly suggests that this transition was something I was fully intended to experience.

Having now experienced this type of transition in separate visions in different directions, the obvious question is whether I would be able at some point to maintain my awareness in both directions, from Threshold into I-Maginal consciousness and back again. Michael Harner's shamanic training teaches that it is very important for practitioners to explicitly experience both the entry and exit from visionary realms in order to guarantee their successful departure and returns.

The Hub motif is a different kind of transition, indicating the availability of travel to multiple destination points. In my experience it appears in visions at a transitional point between one thematic narrative and another, typically using imagery from the Formal realm. It tells the practitioner that a dimensional change is about to occur. It also indicates the presence of a portal that has to be successfully navigated before the practitioner can continue on the visionary path to a new realm.

The symbolic portal within the Hub motif indicates the existence of a smooth bridge between the two realms of different thematic narratives. It allows what normally would be a discontinuous jump between levels to become a smooth transition along a continuous path. Separate thematic narratives can thus become integrated components of a larger, more encompassing scenario, which could describe one possible version of a spiritual journey along the Tao.

This type of transition between thematic narratives represents a third example of seamless integration. It joins the previously discussed examples of transitions between visionary experiences within a realm and between adjacent states of consciousness.

Just as the pixelization phenomenon made me explicitly aware of the transition from one type of consciousness to another, this vision's gateway-like content showed that I'm about to leave one thematic narrative and realm for another. I was now ready to make the jump, both literally and figuratively, into the next realm in my journey, finally leaving behind the domains of the Home realm. My Soul had finally judged me ready to venture into the deeper waters of the Tao.

My journey will resume in the second book of the *American Tao* series, coming later this year.

20: What Comes Next

The Journey through the World Levels

In my next book I will resume the story of my journey as I leave the Home realm of my initial visions and begin a circuit through the three levels of the mystic Worlds. I'll chronicle my shamanic journeys from the familiar surroundings of the Surface World down to the primitive regions of the Under World, where I witness strange beings and rituals. I then travel upwards to the Mountain and High Desert realms of the Upper World, where I undergo a series of trials and tribulations before receiving a magical key and entry into strange societies.

In each world I will pass through two different realms, where I will face different challenges and opportunities for growth. In five of these six realms I will again meet up with the Teacher figure, who will continue to challenge me with a variety of strange sights. Unlike my experiences in the first book, in many of these new visions I will adopt completely different identities and personas, and in a few cases I will take the form of animals. In this second book I will truly begin my journey of revelation and redemption through the many realms of the Soul's Worlds.

The I Ching

Starting in this second book, I will be introducing elements from the ancient Chinese work the *I Ching*, known also as the *Book of Changes*. The *I Ching* discusses how changing configurations of Yin and Yang energies drive an evolving cycle of transformation in the events of the inner and outer worlds. I will be using its principles to assess the different states of my Soul as I travel through my visionary journey. This quick introduction will help you read the annotations I've added to the list of visions that will be discussed in the next book. You can find more information on the meaning of these annotations in one of the many excellent volumes on the *I Ching* that are available (Huang 2010). I will be providing much more detail in the second book.

Each vision will be associated with a particular *I Ching* chapter number (#) and associated six-lined hexagram, which is composed of two trigram elements, with each trigram containing different combinations of three solid (1) or dashed (0) lines. The resulting eight trigrams represent different configurations of Yin (0) and Yang (1) energy, with each associated with a different natural force, symbolized as heaven (111), water (010), mountain (100), thunder (001), wind (110), fire (101), earth (000), and lake (011), as well as other kinds of states and attributes. There are 64 possible hexagram combinations composed from all the possible ways of combining these trigrams. Each hexagram will be used to represent the stage in the Soul's evolutionary journey that was expressed by the symbolism and contents of a given vision.

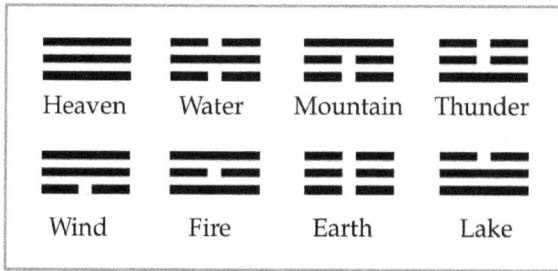

Fig. 19. The Eight Trigrams

Listing of Visions

The following lists the narratives and visions that will be discussed in the next book. It includes the associated *I Ching* chapter number, the chapter's hexagram name, and the associated trigram pairing for each vision. In total thirty-eight new visions will be presented in this book.

Visions in the Surface World

The Spirit Alchemy Narrative in the Forest realm

- "The First Flight", *I Ching* hexagram #20: Watching, Wind/Earth
- "Snow Falls", *I Ching* hexagram #26: Great Accumulation, Mountain/Heaven

165

- "The Pilgrimage", *I Ching* hexagram #17: Following, Lake/Thunder
- "The Melding", *I Ching* hexagram #45: Collecting, Lake/Earth
- "The Rising", *I Ching* hexagram #14: Great Harvest, Fire/Heaven
- "The Burning Trees", *I Ching* hexagram #50: The Cauldron, Fire/Wind

The Spirit Baptismal Narrative in the Ocean realm

- "The Tempest", *I Ching* hexagram #59: Dispersing, Wind/Water
- "The Deep Blue", *I Ching* hexagram #55: Abundance, Thunder/Fire
- "Golden Waves", *I Ching* hexagram #13: Seeking Harmony, Heaven/Fire

Visions in the Under World

The Lost World Narrative in the Jungle realm

- "Down the Rabbit Hole", *I Ching* hexagram #36: Brilliance Injured, Earth/Fire
- "The Jungle Trek", *I Ching* hexagram #19: Approaching, Earth/Lake
- "The Swamp Dragon", *I Ching* hexagram #44: Encountering, Heaven/Wind
- "Mother Protectress", *I Ching* hexagram #18: Remedying, Mountain/Wind
- "The Well of Souls", *I Ching* hexagram #61: Innermost Sincerity, Wind/Lake
- "A Choice of Paths", *I Ching* hexagram #15: Humbleness, Earth/Mountain

The Hidden Source Narrative in the Cave Realm

- "The Three Sisters", *I Ching* hexagram #8: Accord, Water/Earth
- "The Ritual", *I Ching* hexagram #37: The Clan, Wind/Fire
- "The Dark Pool", *I Ching* hexagram #38: Estrangement, Fire/Lake
- "The River Gorge", *I Ching* hexagram #60: Discipline, Eater/Lake
- "The Light Above", *I Ching* hexagram #40, Liberation, Thunder/Water
- "The Blockade", *I Ching* hexagram #12: Hindrance, Heaven/Earth

- "The World Tree", *I Ching* hexagram #53: Develop Gradually, Wind/Mountain

Visions in the Upper World

The Castle Redemption Narrative in the Mountain realm

- "The River Valley", *I Ching* hexagram #4: Childhood, Mountain/Water
- "The Cliff's Edge", *I Ching* hexagram #42: Increase, Wind/Thunder
- "The Peasant's Run", *I Ching* hexagram #33: Retreat, Heaven/Mountain
- "Drafted to Service", *I Ching* hexagram #62: Little Exceeding, Thunder/Mountain
- "The Warrior's Challenge", *I Ching* hexagram #6: Contention, Heaven/Water
- "Empowering the King", *I Ching* hexagram #48: Replenishing, Water/Wind
- "The Golden Key", *I Ching* hexagram #9: Little Accumulation, Wind/Heaven
- "The Clockworks Gate", *I Ching* hexagram #49: Abolishing the Old, Lake/Fire

The Pyramid Advancement Narrative in the High Desert realm

- "The Light Within", *I Ching* hexagram #25: Without Falsehood, Heaven/Thunder
- "The Village of Adepts", *I Ching* hexagram #7: The Multitude, Earth/Water
- "The Selection", *I Ching* hexagram #32: Perseverance, Thunder/Wind
- "The Dragon Clan", *I Ching* hexagram #34: Great Strength, Thunder/Heaven
- "The Golden Corridor", *I Ching* hexagram #10: Treading, Heaven/Lake
- "The White Tower", *I Ching* hexagram #56: The Wanderer, Fire/Mountain
- "The Council of Elders", *I Ching* hexagram #24: Turning Back, Earth/Thunder
- "Lights in the Dark", I Ching hexagram #31: Mutual Influence, Lake/Mountain

Closing Remarks

As I end this first volume, my sincere thanks go out to all of you who have given me some of your lives by reading my words. I know that there are many other spiritual guidebooks out there you could have been reading instead of my story. I hope you have found something in my words that inspired you and will motivate you to begin your own meditative practice, if you do not already have one. If you do, my hope is that my efforts will suggest some ways for you to establish a better dialogue with your Soul and explore the mysteries of the lessons it has to teach.

I have something to ask of you before you go. Actually, there are two things. Both involve writing something. The first asks that you please visit this book's *Amazon* page and write an honest review that expresses your thoughts about this book. Tell me what resonated with you and what else you would like to see explored in subsequent volumes. Please share your thoughts with me by email as well.

My second request is directed at those of you who have had similar experiences to mine but for whatever reasons haven't chosen to write about them. Please do and if you can, share them with others. I know these experiences are deeply personal and sometimes troubling. But the truths these experiences reveal are important and need to be shared, if only to let others like you know they are not alone. You will learn much about yourself in the telling of your stories, as will those of us privileged to share in them. Each of us only sees one side of a many faceted truth; other testimonies can strengthen the message's power. People need to know they are much more than just what they see in the mirror.

So if you are able, please start writing. I would love to read what you have to say. If I can help you in any way, please feel free to contact me. You can write me directly at:

stevos2000@icloud.com

I look forward to hearing from you.

Bibliography

Aurobindo, Sri. *Savitri, A Legend and a Symbol.* Twin Lakes, WI: Lotus Light Publications, 1995.

—. *The Life Divine.* Pondicherry: Sri Aurobindo Ashram, 2010.

Austin, James H. *Zen and the Brain.* Cambridge, MA: The MIT Press, 1999.

Chuang-Tzu. *Basic Writings.* Translated by Burton Watson. New York: Columbia University Press, 1964.

Harner, Michael. *Cave and Cosmos.* Berkeley, CA: North Atlantic Books, 2013.

Hillman, James. *Anima, An Anatomy of a Personified Notion.* Dallas, TX: Spring Publications, Inc., 1993.

—. *Archetypal Psychology, A Brief Account.* Dallas, TX: Spring Publications, Inc., 1988.

Huang, Alfred. *The Complete I Ching, The Definitive Translation.* Rochester, VT: Inner Traditions, 2010.

Huxley, Aldous. *The Perennial Philosophy.* New York: Harper Perennial Modern Classics, 2009.

Jung, C. G. *Memories, Dreams, Reflections.* Revised Edition. Edited by Aniela Jaffe. Translated by Richard and Clara Winston. New York: Vintage Books, 1989.

—. *The Archetypes and the Collective Unconscious.* Second Edition. Translated by R. F. C. Hull. Princeton, NJ: Princeton University Press, 1969.

—. *The Collected Works.* Translated by R.F.C. Hull. Princeton, NJ: Princeton University Press, 1953.

—. *The Red Book, Liber Novus.* Edited by Sonu Shamdasani. Translated by Mark Kyburz, John Peck and Sonu Shamdasani. New York: W.W. Norton & Company, 2009.

Lao-Tzu. *Tao Te Ching.* Translated by Victor H. Mair. New York: Bantam Books, 1990.

—. *Tao Teh Ching.* Edited by Paul K. T. Sih. Translated by John C. H. Wu. New York: St. John's University Press, 1977.

—. *Taoteching.* Translated by Red Pine. Port Townsend, WA: Copper Canyon Press, 2009.

—. *The Tao Te Ching.* Translated by Ellen M. Chen. St. Paul: Paragon House, 1989.

McGilchrist, Iain. *The Master and his Emissary.* New Haven, CT: Yale University Press, 2010.

Pessl, Marisha. *Special Topics in Calamity Physics.* New York: Penguin Books, 2007.

Pocket, Susan. *The Nature of Consciousness: A Hypothesis.* New York: Writers Club Press, 2000.

Skrbina, David. *Panpsychism in the West.* Cambridge, MA: The MIT Press, 2007.

Van Vrekhem, Georges. *Beyond Man.* New Delhi: Rupa Co, 2007.

Whitehead, Alfred North. *Process and Reality.* Corrected Edition. Edited by David Ray Griffin and Donald W. Sherburne. New York: The Free Press, 1985.

Wilber, Ken. *Sex, Ecology, Spirituality.* Second Edition, Revised. Boston: Shambhala, 2000.

Wilhelm, Richard. *The I Ching or Book of Changes.* Translated by Carl F. Baynes. Princeton: Princeton University Press, 1997.

Wittgenstein, Ludwig. *Tractatus Logico-Philosophicus.* Translated by C. K. Ogden. New York: Dover Publications, 1998.

Wong, Eva. *The Shambhala Guide to Taoism.* Boston: Shambhala, 1997.

www.ingramcontent.com/pod-product-compliance
Lightning Source LLC
Chambersburg PA
CBHW052043090426
42739CB00010B/2035